enCharge:

Transform Your Life from Within
Through Your Life Success Factors

by SanDee Priser

Emery Press, LLC
Fort Lauderdale, FL
https://emerypressbooks.com/

First Edition – May 2020

ISBN (Print): 978-0-9600505-4-3
ISBN (ebook): 978-0-9600505-5-0

Editing by Grammar Goddess Editing
Cover design by Sweet 15 Designs

To my nieces, MacKenzie, Delainey, Morgan and Kendra, who I hope are always enCharge of their lives in their own unique ways.

Contents

Chapter 1 – Drifting

"A life without attention to detail is like a
perfectly maintained straight highway – safe
and predictable, but completely uninspiring."

EVERYONE CALLED ME "DOC" because I knew from an early age that I was going to be an orthopedic surgeon.

Except I ended up getting a business degree.

Through a music scholarship.

And am now licensed to practice law.

Was I confused? Overconfident? Unfocused? Clueless? Perhaps all of these and more at different times. But I was opportunistic in seeking out the things that were interesting, energizing, and that fully engaged me. And doing so has led me to a life that is nothing I had expected and yet is very satisfying and fulfilling.

I want to help you be an opportunist (in a good way), too, and put yourself on the path to achieving dreams you may not even realize you have. And that's why I'm writing this book. But I'm getting ahead of myself.

Despite my carefully plotted plans for medical school and beyond, some events in high school caused me to reassess what I was doing and consider entirely different directions. Yes, plural. Mine was not a direct path, but one with several twists and turns. I might not have realized it at the time, but that was a good thing because those changes in direction helped me realize the value of both embracing opportunities that presented themselves and, later, creating opportunities I wanted but didn't exist.

I'd been happily working my way through life up until high school. Well, that's not quite true. "Working" suggests that I had a goal in mind, some sort of plan. And other than declaring I'd be an orthopedic surgeon, I was just going with the flow and being grateful for wherever that took me. I'd grown up knowing I was loved and loving others (even if I often said I hated my two older brothers and would never talk to them again), but it was also clear that despite how hard both of my parents worked, we didn't have much money. I'd put us squarely in "upper lower class," if there is such a class.

What perhaps distinguished us in that class is that both of my parents had college degrees and understood the value of education. Dad had a degree in agriculture and was, not surprisingly, a farmer. Mom, meanwhile, had a degree in business education and during my childhood had taught business education (e.g., keyboarding, bookkeeping, office procedures and shorthand[1]) as well as worked in various secretarial (what we'd now call executive assistant) positions. There was always the expectation that the three of us could, and generally should, get a college education, but we would have to work for it (or borrow a good chunk of change).

If you grow up on a farm, work is a part of your daily life. From an early age, there were chores for all of us and a

---

[1] *You might not have heard of shorthand. It is FASCINATING. I remain intrigued to this day. Look it up and tell me these quasi-modern hieroglyphics don't have a role in combatting something in much the way that the Navajo code talkers worked in World War 2.*

fair amount of rules. One rule, for example, was, "You don't eat until the animals eat." In addition to the beef cattle we had for some years, we also had lots of barn cats, a small poodle (yes, on a farm – it's a long story), and a rabbit named Smutz, and all of them needed to be fed.

You'd think Smutz would be the easy chore because his hutch was right outside the garage whereas the cats were all the way out in the barn. The catch with Smutz, though, is that except when there was snow on the ground (another rule), you fed him not by pouring out pellets and doling out hay, but by picking grass for him by hand, which was a chilly task for tiny hands when there was thick frost (and which often resulted in me showing up at school with grass stains on my hands). But it was character building, particularly in learning that often in life you need to put others first and be a bit patient when it comes to your own desires.[2]

Growing up on an Illinois farm in the 1980s, there weren't neighborhood kids right next door to play with, so I often had to entertain myself. Given the relative level of isolation and my brothers being my primary playmates, it was perhaps inevitable that I became a tomboy (though I did torment kittens by dressing them up and, in my horse-crazy years, sewing "saddle blankets" for them and teaching them to jump over barriers). I remember playing with miniature farm implements and hauling popcorn kernels around in

---

[2] *My parents may have been leadership gurus ahead of their time. An interesting read is Simon Sinek's,* Leaders Eat Last: Why Some Teams Pull Together and Others Don't, *which didn't come out until nearly 40 years after I was carrying out my morning duties.*

small gravity beds and using the small auger to take them from point A to point B. This seemed normal to me.

My brothers were adamant that, in addition to learning the finer points of transporting popcorn kernels, I learn to play all of the sports offered at our small school so that I wouldn't embarrass them (and for which I will always be grateful, though it was awkward at times when I was chosen on teams ahead of boys). So, we'd toss around a softball or football while waiting for the school bus, play games of "P-I-G" or "H-O-R-S-E" with the basketball hoop in the barn, etc. I also attempted to learn to play tennis by using an old wooden racquet of Mom's, whacking a similarly old tennis ball against the side of the barn in a (clean) part of the cow lot. In a nutshell, I was super classy, but it was how I grew up and I enjoyed the variety.

Another set of rules was that we should be grateful for what we had (even if it wasn't much), there was no place for whining or complaining, and you needed to learn to suck it up when things got tough. When I was 11 or 12, I was playing with some friends in the high school gym which had a (very unforgiving) cement floor. While running for a ball, I collided with others and we got tangled in a heap with my foot twisted somewhere in between. I continued to play, but it *really* hurt. A neighbor gave me a ride home that night and I went to school the next day as usual. When it was time to go to church over the weekend, cramming my foot into my black patent leather Mary Janes was really painful and I mentioned it (okay, whined) to Mom. Wrong approach. She told me to suck it up (not in so many words) and get in the car.

Afterwards, as I was taking off said shoes and my awesome cable knit cotton tights, I pointed out to Mom that the strap from the one shoe had created a neat racing stripe across my foot. Which is to say, it was horribly swollen, and the strap had left a clean line through it. She realized then it was an issue. Yeah, turned out my foot was broken. (Mom still feels bad about this, but she got me into the doctor and my foot healed just fine.)

But the most important skill I learned as a kid was reading, which opened an entire new world to me. We lived about 15 minutes from the nearest town and once a month Mom would take us to the library. It was magical. Entering the library felt like entering a church, both because it was still and quiet, and because I had such reverence for the rows and rows of books. The special area in the basement for kids. The coat hooks that hinted you were welcome to take off your parka and stay a while. The reading area with little brightly colored chairs for story time. The smell of paper mixed with the musty scent of slushy snow boots in the corner. Hardcovers wrapped in plastic sleeves. The swishing sound of pages turning as people read. Dewey decimal stickers indicating that every single volume had a special place. A paper slip in the inside that gave you an idea of the last time someone had opened that book. I was so jealous of those librarians getting to spend the **entire day** there. The only thing missing was a crackling fireplace to make it my geek version of Nirvana, though even I realized that paper and sparks don't mix well.

According to Mom, I got at least four books each visit, always including a biography and a book about a topic that I didn't know anything about. Hardy Boys or Nancy Drew books were verboten because they were mysteries, which were somehow bad for me (I borrowed those from my friend, Omar, and read them while at school so Mom didn't find out). This love of learning has stuck with me my entire life and I still *try* to read at least one non-fiction book per week.

Since we only went to the library once per month, I often ran out of books and read pretty much anything I could get my hands on. Since there was no internet, that meant reading things as mundane as cereal boxes or whatever came in the mail. Sometime in junior high, Mom subscribed to *Working Woman* magazine, and I started devouring them even though I was neither working nor a full-fledged woman at the time. They stopped publishing the magazine in 2001, but it was primarily targeted to women in white collar positions, often pictured wearing navy suits with blouses featuring floppy bows (hey, it was the '80s) and looking rather successful and confident.

What a coincidence. I want to be successful and confident, too. But tomboy that I am, not sure about those bows....

I added "research" to my library activities and started researching the jobs noted in the magazine and even noted a few that were interesting, even though I "knew" I was going to be an orthopedic surgeon.[3] Through reading, I became comfortable wading into areas where I didn't know exactly what was going on so that I could learn what WAS going on.

---

[3] *In retrospect, reading about the issues that women often faced on the job probably made me more attuned to potential career and working relationship issues, so I was able to avoid at least some of them.*

It was one of those few areas in life where there was all upside (learning more) and no downside to a research "failure." And through it, I became relatively facile in a variety of areas, whether they were relevant to my daily life or not.[4] Unfortunately, chemistry was not one of those areas.

In elementary school and junior high I'd always earned good grades that placed me at or near the top of my (admittedly relatively small) class. Sure, I preferred reading, writing and spelling to math and science, but I was fine with the latter topics, too. In junior high, I had the misfortune to have my first knee arthroscopy and became fascinated with orthopedic surgery. The surgeon was a bit goofy but had a great way of explaining what was going on and what he was going to do. And he had a Porsche with the custom license plate, SAW BONZ – what's not to like? That's when I decided that I would be an orthopedic surgeon. I told all my friends about this plan, started writing "Dr. Priser" in a dreamy way not unlike how a more, um, normal girl might write in flowery cursive with hearts for I's in her name or tag on the last name of the boyfriend she was swooning about, and others started calling me Doc. I knew where I was going and was full of confidence when I entered high school.

And that confidence persisted through my first year of high school when I earned an A in biology class. But chemistry my sophomore year was an entirely different

---

[4] *There's a growing field of research that indicates that the value of learning and doing a variety of things can be very helpful in being creating and innovative in a constantly changing world. A great introduction to the topic is David Epstein's* Range: Why Generalists Triumph in a Specialized World. *I find his comparison between the backgrounds and experiences of Tiger Woods and Roger Federer particularly fascinating.*

matter. I got a B. My first B. Ever. I know, cry me a river, but it was really upsetting to me at the time as I had never encountered something that I couldn't do well (I would argue now that a B was still doing well, but that would have been little consolation to me at the time). And I decided that if I couldn't do chemistry, then I – obviously! – couldn't be a physician.

So, this was a bit of a setback. But it was only temporary because I had still been developing in other areas that allowed me to switch my energy and focus to other things that interested me. I was progressing in music. I was reading *Working Woman* before Mom even realized it had arrived in the mail. I was playing a variety of intramural sports (softball, flag football, floor hockey, volleyball) and not embarrassing my brothers. And I was becoming more and more fascinated with business.

I took after my Mom as I was a whiz at typing (clocked about 120 words per minute, thanks, no doubt, to years of piano lessons) and also enjoyed office procedures and bookkeeping. But I looked at the financial state of my parents and knew I wanted something more than what Mom was doing.

The high school I attended was unique in that we went to class half a day and worked the other half, usually for teachers grading papers or other similar jobs. The coveted jobs were the higher-paying ones off campus, but you had to be at least 16 years old before you could apply for them. So, the summer after I turned 16, I applied for and was hired at Richardson Electronics, Ltd. I worked in the warehouse area, got to wear jeans – the steel-toed shoes were less exciting –

and was part of a two-person team processing goods returned from customers. It was a great introduction to the practicalities of how businesses function, both the literal hands-on work and use of IT systems and concepts I'd learn later in university like inventory control, production, and warehouse operations. I felt like I was starting to understand what I'd been reading about for years in *Working Woman*.

A year or so later, I worked my way up to a cushy office job in Purchasing as a file clerk (no steel-toed shoes, though I was less excited about trading my jeans in for skirts). This position expanded my knowledge of business and also gave me my first taste of responsibility – I was handed what, in retrospect, was the least important role in Purchasing -- office supplies for the headquarters location. But it was mine and I was terribly proud.

Laugh all you want, but as a high school kid, the idea that I could order stuff and have the company pay for it was a heady experience. I particularly enjoyed it when departments had orders for special items that required something other than re-stocking the standard items. I learned to keep available stock limited during back-to-school days (seriously, people, you're stealing for your kids?!), got to try out new products that the vendor was introducing, and had people asking what I would recommend for certain products. Me? Yeah.

So, I started steering people to the brands I preferred. I won't say I was an influencer in the sense of social media today, but, for example, I was shameless in promoting (with no compensation) Bates staplers. I thought they were not only more pleasing from a design perspective and available in cool

'80s colors (dusty blue or putty, anyone?), but they were less expensive than Swingline, would not easily be stolen by others as they were more unique, *and* they had a LIFETIME warranty (this was clearly before Milton from the *Office Space* movie made the red Swingline a bit more cult).

There was another task in the purchasing clerk position that didn't seem like much of an opportunity at the time. We occasionally received listings (often many typed pages long) of products that other companies (usually smaller entities) had available for sale. These weren't formal catalogs, but more like odds and ends that they wanted to unload, many with only one or two items available – maybe a primitive version of Overstock or eBay. Someone decided that it would be great if we could put all of those items and available quantities into a large spreadsheet so that they would be searchable. Okay.

Now, again, this was the late '80s – there were no network directories, let alone SharePoint sites or cloud storage. So, it was all on a standalone desktop computer. None of the full-time employees wanted to spend their valuable time entering the information, so it naturally fell to me as the clerk. Okay, so I put my 120 word-per-minute typing skills to work and cranked out these lists, making it a game to see how much I could accomplish and to try to get through all of the lists that had piled up.

As I progressed, I grew really curious about what spreadsheets were and what one could do with them. At the time, Lotus 1-2-3 was the spreadsheet of choice because Microsoft Office didn't exist yet. In fact, Windows didn't even exist until 1993, about five years later. None of the full-time employees really understood Lotus 1-2-3, either, other than basic entry and searching. I convinced them to buy a book on the topic. I pored through it and started creating formulas to really leverage the tool. I became the Lotus 1-2-3 expert with rumors of my geekiness even spreading to other groups who sought me out for help. I really enjoyed that mini-consulting role. So, I converted a mindless, thankless task into an opportunity to establish a knowledge base and a bit of geek reputation. Not bad for a high school-aged tomboy still trying to learn how-to walk-in pumps.

So, by this time, I had transitioned from a surgeon wannabe to being fascinated and engaged with business and well on my way to seeking a business degree in college. I was happily drifting along and enjoying the ride. And then one of the other doors I had kept open drew me in.

Way back in elementary school (second grade, to be specific) I'd started learned to play the piano and added clarinet in fifth grade.[5] It quickly became clear that I was much better at clarinet than I was at piano. Granted, a lot of that was because soooooo many people play the piano and not many take wind instrument performance all that seriously. Nevertheless, in my admittedly small high school, my clarinet skills were outstanding relative to my peers. In fact, at a certain point, the high school band director who had

---

[5] *I am forever grateful for having the gift of music lessons and still have no idea how my parents afforded them. Research continues to show that music learning can have a direct impact on brain structure and intellectual development. There is a lot of information out there, though one of the more recent studies I have seen was from USC's Brain and Creativity Institute, the link to which indicates the overall results: https://news.usc.edu/102681/childrens-brains-develop-faster-with-music-training/*

been teaching me how to play the clarinet admitted I probably wouldn't learn anything more from him. My mom somehow figured out a way (and budget) for me to take lessons from Mel, a professor at a local public university, Northern Illinois University (NIU).

In addition to being an amazing teacher, Mel was a serious clarinetist, having performed with the Chicago Symphony Orchestra (the standard against which I measure all orchestras, I confess) and many other major symphonies. So, the fact that NIU might not be one of the higher profile universities in the nation didn't diminish the fact that I was in the company of an amazing musician. And he pulled no punches. Recall that I had grown up with two older brothers, so I was used to them and others being very direct with and critical of me. But I'd had such a relatively easy time with my clarinet study because there wasn't much competition that I had gotten, well, a bit full of myself. Mel punctured that ego balloon, and rather quickly.

I learned later from Mom that he agreed to my auditioning for him only after she badgered him relentlessly. He thought she was just another proud mother who might be a BIT biased as to the skill of her child. But apparently, he agreed that I had some talent. To be clear, that message was not at all apparent in our first lessons. I remembered vividly him sighing a bit in our first lesson and saying, somewhat exasperatedly, "Where to start?"

He started by breaking down everything I had been so carefully building up. First, he wanted me to learn how to properly breathe. I wondered if that was some kind of a joke because, well, OBVIOUSLY, I knew how to breathe. "Clearly you don't, or we wouldn't be having this conversation. And until you can breathe in and out, you cannot make your instrument speak and have a conversation with the audience."

Clearly this was going to be a bit different than what I was used to.

My assignment the first week was to practice my breathing with various exercises, both to breathe in as well as to how to control how, when and how much to exhale. I got rather lightheaded from all of it. And I was pretty sure he was crazy and wasting Mom's hard-earned money. At the second week's lesson, he reviewed my work, nodded, and said, "Better. Keep practicing."

He added to my assignment for the following week scales and arpeggios. That's it. No "real" music. This went on for well over a month. Then he added some short pieces that were less like real pieces and more like exercises with a little variation, but it was something slightly different. Meanwhile, I was continuing to play in band, so I had some other outlets.

What was interesting, though, was that from the beginning, we would end each lesson by playing some sort of duet together. It seemed a bit like a reward at the time, and perhaps it was, but it was also a way for him to see how my skills, sight-reading, and pattern-recognition were developing. Because what he was doing – and I was too immature to know – was that by breaking my "game" down to its fundamentals, he was setting the foundation for rapid growth in the future. By focusing on my breathing and breath control, I was improving my sound. By working on scales and arpeggios, I was hard wiring into my brain and fingers the building blocks of every piece of music out there. So, it became a pattern-recognition exercise – once I knew the patterns, I could pick up a piece of music and play most of it right off the bat. When it all started coming together, I was amazed. And every lesson ended with that nod and, "Better. Keep practicing."

So, I was improving and felt that I was, despite the reality check from Mel, pretty good at the clarinet, but I couldn't see that being a career option for me. I liked music, yes, and the social aspects. But I wasn't as passionate about it as "real" musicians I knew; music seemed to be the core and essence of their being. I wasn't there. I was more passionate about succeeding, getting to the head of the pack and using music to get there. A sort of passive-aggressive competition for the intellectually or artistically inclined.

I'd developed a keen sense of competition but felt more comfortable competing in more intellectual pursuits rather than sports. I enjoyed competing for the top clarinet spot, had started playing in the high school band when I was only in 6th grade, moved my way up to first chair clarinet by my sophomore year in high school and basically kept it until I graduated.[6] So it was fun and served a purpose, created a

---

[6] *Okay, time out for transparency. My junior year in high school, a classmate -- and friend -- of mine edged me out for first chair in auditions at the beginning of the school year. I was like, "What?! How could that happen?" There was a process where you could "challenge" someone for their chair. So, um, I challenged her for the seat. And won. And basically, ruined a friendship over it. She literally wouldn't talk to me for a few months. We pretty much patched things up before we graduated, but we were never close again. So I ruined a good friendship because of my ego. I did learn from the experience, but too late. Don't be a jerk like I was. Compete. Accept the outcome. And then train so that you do better in the next competition.*

really collaborative team atmosphere and I made some great friends on the trips we took to perform in various parts of the state. But a career (or, to be perfectly honest, a job that would be likely to put me in a decent financial position)? Ehh....

Pursuing a degree in business seem much more logical. Initially, I thought maybe marketing (by which I probably really meant advertising) because it seemed flashy and glamorous, but I wasn't sure I was creative enough. Finance? Meh. My high school yearbook from my senior year (I was the editor, natch) lists my career ambition as Vice President of Marketing or Finance and my secret ambition was to play with the Chicago Symphony Orchestra or teach at Harvard Business School. Clearly, I was still confused. But then I heard about a new niche career -- music merchandising.

Sounds interesting. Maybe a good way to combine my interests in music and business? But what IS it?

The leading university at the time (perhaps still today) was the University of Miami (not to be confused with Miami University in Ohio), which was a long way from home, a private school, and, naturally, expensive. I'd done enough reading to know that many, if not most, college students change their major at least once, so the idea of shelling out a lot of cash (or, more likely, adding on a lot of college debt) for something that I wasn't 100 percent sure about sounded like an expensive way to experiment.

I asked Mel for advice. "Well, look, why don't you go to college here at NIU? You can continue taking lessons from me. We've got both a great music program and a good business school. So, you can take your core business courses in a bit more stable situation and, if you decide you really want to do music merchandising, you can get your Master's in that. But maybe you'll find on the way that you want to do music, or you want to do business, a major, minor, etc. You have more options." Made sense.

So, I applied and was accepted to NIU for my freshman year and everything he said about music and business were spot on. But at the same time, I felt a bit lost and overwhelmed. I was one of some 12,000 undergrads at NIU, which was a bit of a culture shock coming from a high school of a couple hundred. Being involved in the honors program and a music ensemble helped me find environments where I could get to know some people, but I felt a little like a fish out of water. It was also, even after several years of lessons with Mel, a reality check, as I was definitely not the top dog anymore, so I wasn't getting that feeling of success and achievement that I'd gotten from music in the past. And, you know, business school wasn't exactly easy.

So, I found myself kind of drifting, going through the motions to keep my head above water, but not really driven by or to something I was passionate about. And I certainly hadn't given any more thought to music merchandising. I was too busy to even think about whether I was happy, which pretty much means that I wasn't. And the things that had energized me in high school – intramural sports, reading for fun, promoting Bates staplers etc. – weren't present, so I didn't have a connection to things that made me feel like, well, "me."

And then an opportunity arose that I had neither been looking for nor expecting but, in retrospect, I had set in motion years before. When I started taking clarinet lessons back in 5th grade, it was from the band director of the private high school that I would attend later. He saw potential in me and, a year later, wanted to invite me to the band clinic hosted at the high school that was for students in grades 7-12. Since I wasn't yet in the 7th grade, he asked if the conductor/clinician minded. Suffice it to say, the clinician was NOT a fan, noting that the clinic was for serious musicians, not babysitting kids. I could come, but there were no guarantees I would be allowed to stay. Of course, I had no idea about any of this until years later and just knew that I was invited to go to the clinic and was very excited.

I was also slightly intimidated because I did know that I would be one of the youngest there. Both of my brothers would also be participating in the clinic – my oldest brother, a senior, on trumpet, and my sophomore (and also sophomoric) brother on trombone. The clinician was returning and had struck the two of them as very demanding and she really, really pushed them, but they learned a lot.

Hold up. "She?"

"Conductor" had not been covered in *Working Woman*, perhaps because there were so few women in the field at an advanced level. I was fascinated by a woman filling such an important and clear leadership role for the entire ensemble, as well as teaching conducting and other courses at the university level. In any event, the opportunity to play under the direction of a female conductor made me really excited about the clinic. And nervous. Because, um, I'd never played in ANY ensemble before. Had no idea how this really worked. My brothers explained the basics and I practiced my music and showed up and took my place among the masses playing the third clarinet part. It didn't seem particularly difficult as I already knew my music, but it was new to keep an eye on both the music as well as the conductor to make sure I didn't miss something. And I definitely didn't want to be called out like some others in the ensemble were for not paying attention.

We practiced for a grueling day and a half and then had the concert the third night. I really enjoyed it and was hooked on playing in ensembles. Because let's be honest, no one really wants to hear the clarinet by itself – it's more of a team "sport" rather than individual one. I was able to begin playing in the high school band the next year when I was in the 7th grade and also attended the clinic every year until I graduated from high school. The clinician who everyone referred to as "Fav" (a shortened version of her last name, Favorito) returned each year and I got to know her pretty well, to the point that when she left the university where she was teaching to pursue her doctorate in conducting, we became pen pals. She clearly had the patience of a saint to do this as I clearly had nothing to offer her. But as a great teacher, she apparently enjoyed developing promising musicians and I was fortunate to be among those she mentored.

So fast forward, then, to my time at NIU as I was drifting along. Fav and I were still writing back and forth and she asked if I would have any interest in transferring to a small private university in Southern California and, in exchange for a tuition waiver, basically sell my musical soul.

Um, I'm intrigued by the idea of the university equivalent of an all-expense-paid nine-month vacation in sunny California

24

with academic credit. Worst case, I could transfer back at the end of a year if I hate it, right? And I already know I like playing in Fav's ensembles. What do I really have to lose? Tell me more....

The deal was that I would have to play in orchestra, wind ensemble and band, my clarinet lessons would be included and -- get this -- I didn't have to be a music major or even a minor unless I wanted to. That seemed like a good fit. At the same time, though, I'd be going halfway across the country, far away from family, friends and home to a much smaller and less well-known university. But having spent the first year at NIU in the dorm (even though home was close enough I could have commuted), I figured I would be able to downsize to the smaller campus, perhaps make closer friends (let's be honest, I hadn't really made any lasting friends at NIU to that point). So, all things considered, I took a chance and accepted the offer. Doing so helped me kind of bring everything together. I could do music for fun while maintaining my focus on exploring business to find an area that also resonated with me.

Looking back at all of this, I see that up to this point, I had kind of muddled through and let my skills and circumstances form the trajectory of my life. But at the same time, I was continuing to do things that made me connected and fulfilled in small ways and was open to opportunities. When opportunities presented themselves that could take me out of my comfort zone to a place, literally and figuratively, where more of my passions intersected, I considered and pursued them when they made sense. In accepting the music scholarship, I found a way to combine my interests in music and business in a way that was financially advantageous in terms of not coming out of school with a lot of debt.

Why am I telling you about all of this? It is certainly not because I had life all figured out by the time I was in college. Quite the contrary. If I had to do life over again, I would have changed some of the things I tried and didn't try based on what I know now. But I can't. And neither can you. We can only look towards how we live now and how we create the circumstances for an even more fulfilling life in the future.

That's what we're going to explore in the remainder of this book.

Chapter 2 – Life Success Factors

"It doesn't matter how you try to manage your energy if you don't know its source or how to generate more."

ONE OF THE BIGGEST LESSONS I've learned is how important it is to know the interests or pursuits that consistently make you feel fulfilled, satisfied and happy. There are two parts to this. First is the consistency part. I'm not talking about something that makes you happy for a short period of time, like a massage, watching a baby's first halting steps or watching a beautiful sunset. Those are all well and good, but they're also fleeting and quickly forgotten as we have to return to the mundaneness of day-to-day activities. I'm talking about the things you keep coming back to because they energize you and excite your passions and push you to want to do more – and which don't involve drugs, alcohol or other substance to put you in that happy state. That said, there are some things that can make you happy in the short term that also point you towards larger interests. Playing with puppies may give you short-term happiness, but it may also indicate that you have an interest in animals that could transition into something like a career involving animals, a hobby of dog agility training, qualifying your dog as a support animal to help hospital patients, or volunteering at an animal shelter.

The second part is that these are things that make *you* feel happy and fulfilled, not what makes people generally feel happy or what society or social media may suggest **should** make you happy. There is usually a big difference between the two. When you think about what makes you happy and fulfilled, they are feelings that are inside of you. Yes, they may manifest in external activities or things, but they're about something more. Society (including what we see on various media or in advertisements), on the other hand, is almost always talking about things. They not-so-subtly tell us that we should have a fat paycheck, a nice car, a big house, designer clothes, glamorous travel, gourmet food, and on and on. And there is absolutely nothing wrong with any of those things **IF they are part of something much larger driven by** *your own interests* **and life vision.**

I refer to this collection of happiness- and fulfillment-creating interests and passions as Life Success Factors – things that need to be done on a consistent basis to be happy and consider your life a success. Factors may be driven by what you are passionate about, what you are afraid of, what lights you up and more. The list should be relatively short because if these are your essentials, you shouldn't need a big suitcase to carry them.

I started thinking about those activities about the time I was in my late twenties to early thirties. I was trying to decide whether to stay in my current job or leave and practice law and had scored time on the calendar of one of my mentors. She happened to be one of the global leaders for our firm, so her time was really valuable, and I didn't want to waste it. As I planned for the meeting, I tried visualizing how it might play out (always a good practice). It seemed reasonable for her to ask what would make me happy and then tie that back to whether that might be more likely if I stayed at the firm or left. So, I wrote on the back of an index card (which I still have) what I now refer to as my Life Success Factors:

- Active exploration
- Teaching
- Health
- Creativity
- Financial security

If you'll allow me some truthiness and transparency, I'll break these down so you can understand why I've been sharing all of these random stories.

- **Active exploration.** You might be tempted to say, "That's just consultant-speak for 'learning'" and you'd be somewhat right. Because it's not just about learning, but actively driving the learning, rather than being in a passive state. Letting my curiosity lead me and being curious about life in general. In most of our formal education, we are told what we must learn, though the higher you progress the more choice you may have on those options. Active exploration is about seeking out what's interesting to me. It's checking out that library book about a topic I know nothing about. It's about snagging *Working Woman* out of the mailbox to see what's inside. It's about asking whether there's a better option for a stapler. It's about learning Lotus 1-2-3 when all I *needed* to do was enter data.

- **Teaching.** Teaching is the flipside of learning because you can't teach (at least effectively) what you don't know. For me, it's taking what I've learned and find fascinating and repackaging it to share with others who might find it interesting, too. It's not just teaching in a classroom setting, though I really enjoy that, too (hello, Harvard Business School secret ambition). Teaching can also be as simple as a conversation over lunch, coaching a colleague through a tricky problem, a blog or social media post, or any other medium where I can share what I've learned. And the great part about teaching is that, particularly if you make it an interactive experience, it not only reinforces the information in your own brain, but also creates a collaborative environment where questions from others may lead to deeper understanding and more – you guessed it – active exploration.

- **Health.** You can get more done in life if you're healthy, both physically and mentally. Yes, unhealthy people can do amazing things, too, but health makes it easier for you to explore, to have more energy to accomplish tasks, to live longer, and myriad other benefits. My family medical history is rife with cancer, tumors and heart disease, so I want to have a healthy lifestyle in order to either avoid these diseases altogether, or to be better situated to fight them if they come. Health issues also had a significant influence on my family as my father was diagnosed with multiple sclerosis when I was a senior in high school. This very healthy man went from strapping farmer to not being able to walk, even with a walker or cane, by the time I graduated from college. While that was not something that, at least with the current knowledge of the disease, could have been prevented, it reminds me of the importance of health in accomplishing what we can while we are still able. But health is not just absence of disease or maintaining a healthy weight. It's also about the little things that allow you to achieve peak performance, like getting the right quantity and quality of sleep, eating the right food, balancing cardio and strength training, practicing mindfulness and taking breaks from devices to give your brain a break. And let's face it, if your body is not in good shape, your mental health and ability to regulate your moods and emotions will also be challenging. Once again, my active exploration interest kicks in here as I am always looking for ways to tweak my health.[7]

- **Creativity.** From making up games to amuse myself on the farm to writing poetry in junior high (usually signed "Dr. Priser") to various musical endeavors, creativity has always been important to me. It's not

---

[7] *For example, as I write this, one of my goals is to achieve three hours total of REM (rapid eye movement) and deep sleep and minimum of an hour each. It is not easy and I'm not doing well so far, though I am tracking it and see some improvements already. But I know that focusing on this will allow my body to repair, my brain to reinforce learning and to awake refreshed.*

something that is my focus, but it's a way for me to relax. I've written silly stories for friends, a parable about the Sarbanes-Oxley Act of 2002, a poem about my first Audi (which hung at one point in time on the wall of my dealer) and Christmas stories for my nieces when they were younger. But there are other outlets for creativity as well – developing an innovative proposal for a client, creating a compelling training session on a topic that otherwise seems a bit dry (see also Sarbanes-Oxley Act of 2002), structuring collaborative team environments, or trying to create a bird feeder that is both squirrel and bear-proof, for example.

- **Financial security.** Now that you know a bit about my background growing up upper lower class and the additional financial challenges posed by my father's disability, you can see why this is important to me. Note that I didn't specify that I want wealth (though that's certainly welcome); rather I want stability that will provide me with a consistent income for paying my bills and planning for retirement. With that stability, I can then be in a position to pursue other life success factors that could lead to greater financial resources or invest in experiences that make me happy.

So those are what I came up with at the time. I thought they were pretty good and was pleased to present them to my mentor.

Without missing a beat, she asked, "So family and friends aren't important to your life?"

Oh, snap! Yes, yes, they are....

So, I added a sixth life success factor: **meaningful relationships**. This includes, of course, having those relationships, but also is an affirmative obligation to be selective about those relationships. I need to nurture the relationships that I have to make them beneficial for both of us, rather than taking them for granted. I need to recognize that some of my relationships may no longer be meaningful, in that they may either be harmful to me or the other person and need to be exited or we have just grown apart in many ways that it may be best to let them recede. Equally important, though, is to seek out relationships with individuals with whom I share common interests, particularly if those align with my life success factors. Overall, I want to surround myself with people who bring me joy, make me think, do not judge me, are willing to be brutally honest with me, who encourage my growth and for whom I can also do those same things as healthy relationships involve equal parts of giving and receiving.

So, what do life success factors actually *do*?

As the Cheshire Cat noted in *Alice in Wonderland*, "If you don't know where you're going, any road will take you there." In the stories that I have shared, there are instances when I have gone with the flow, drifted and let life happen to me. That can often happen when we are tired or, just as commonly, when we don't have a direction in life. If you have no direction in life, it is impossible to know whether you're going in the right direction and equally impossible to invest your energy productively.

Production and direction of energy is what life success factors are all about. Whether you are thinking about actual electricity or your personal energy, it's true that energy flows through the path of least resistance. Without a plan, your limited and precious energy will just disperse, leaving you to go with the flow and take life as it comes, wondering why you're often not happy or achieving the things you want. But if, instead, you channel your energy, you can plug into the areas that will amplify your energy and direct them towards productive output. Life success factors are those channels.

When you know the things that lead towards lasting happiness and fulfillment, you can then measure opportunities against the life success factors. The better opportunities are the ones that clearly contribute to one or more of the life success factors. When an opportunity arises and it doesn't seem to relate to any of your life success factors, it's probably not one worth considering.

But if you find yourself nevertheless thinking about something, consider whether it's an option or an opportunity. They're often not the same thing.

Options versus Opportunities

Just because we HAVE options doesn't mean we have to choose them. Whether it's free junk food, multiple invitations on a weekend, or ventilated seats on a new car, options presented to us may not always be good or right for us, and we don't have to choose them.

I'm not talking about binary choices like whether to roll over and go back to sleep or get up and go to work – those are choices with consequences and not choosing one means you do the other. No. I'm talking about things that pop up that might seem like opportunities, which may or may not be true. Like a donut truck that appears after you've already had dinner and are satisfied. They're options, but you don't need them, and you might very well regret them later.

Taking the time to pause and consider each option and whether it will benefit you now or in the future, whether it might be harmful, whether it helps move you toward or away from your goals, and whether accepting or rejecting it may cause you regret, can help frame whether the option is truly and opportunity you can't pass up.

A cautionary note: No single life success factor will make you whole. Equally, all life success factors should not be satisfied solely by one particular activity or relationship (for example, your job or marriage). That type of concentration will lead to a lack of wider vision and stagnation of growth because all of your eggs are in one basket. And, of course, should something happen to that job or marriage, for example, it would be nearly catastrophic to your growth and happiness. Rather, the more areas where you touch on one or more of your life success factors will create a diversified base that will allow you to withstand hits to any of those areas because you're receiving fulfillment from multiple components. It is the combination of life success factors that are touched upon repeatedly over time that provide the platform for your growth.

Life success factors are also a great defense against the dreaded FOMO (Fear of Missing Out), because life success factors allow you to accurately predict when you're actually not going to be missing out on something that matters to you versus what you know will make you happy.

You might think that life success factors is just a longer phrase for goals, but they are different. Goals are meant to be achieved. They have an end. Their achievement can be measured. Life success factors, on the other hand, are values that you will pursue throughout your entire life. They may drive goals but are not themselves goals. They will be there to help you make choices as your life changes and new opportunities arise that you must consider. And they may help you decide which goals you may want to set.

Take the example of money. One of my life success factors is financial security. When will that be met? Never, because as long as I am alive, my financial needs and the ability to meet them are constantly being measured. Contrast that with a goal of having a net worth of $5 million by the time I retire. That goal can be achieved (though it also requires a lot of hard work). The goal is consistent with having financial security but is not itself a life success factor.

We will talk more about the practical application of life success factors and how to use them to pursue a life that will make you happy and give you a sense of fulfillment. Understanding your own life success factors is critical for this. Not just for your career, but for how you want to live and the legacy you wish to leave behind.

So, let's talk about *your* life success factors.

Let's be clear – there are no right or wrong life success factors. And your life success factors will probably be very different from mine, because we come from different backgrounds and have our own unique dreams and desires. While many life success factors are driven by dreams, others may be the product of fear, just as my health and financial stability life success factors were driven by fears from my life experiences.[8]

Start by grabbing a blank sheet of paper and divide it into two or three columns and 8-10 rows so you have enough space to write in each of the blocks. An Excel or Word document also works well for this.

Brainstorm a bit and think about the following, writing the events/activities that come to mind in the blocks:

- When you visualize your perfect day, what are you doing? Are there themes? Would the perfect day be the same day five years from now? Would you have also enjoyed that day five years ago?
- Which of your five senses are the most important to you? Why? And when you think of using or experiencing the sense, what are you doing?
- Are there things you started doing earlier in life that you still do, even if you don't know why?

---

[8] *I'm not suggesting here that you let fear drive your life. Just the contrary. Recognize that we all have fears. Our choice is to acknowledge them and define our goals, or allow the fears themselves to define us. The key is growing beyond fears, not allowing fear to limit our growth.*

- Do you miss things you used to do but somehow have stopped doing them?
- Take a look at photos from your life or that box of mementos you probably have stashed somewhere. What positive or joyful memories and events do they bring to mind?
- When you feel a sparkle that lights you up, what is it that you're doing it?
- Think back to major decisions you have made that created an inflection point in your life. Why did you choose them? What was the outcome? Would you do it again? Why or why not?
- What are your fears? Be specific. Vague feelings such as, "What if I'm not good enough?" or "What will everyone else think?" are generally not specific enough to be actionable.

If I took my early years that I described in Chapter 1, my document might have contained things like this:

Table 1

Training kittens, teaching Dynamo Ranger to gallop	Sports with my brothers at the bus stop	Chores on the farm
Better. Keep practicing.	Mentors like Mel, Fav	Choosing books on topics about which I knew nothing
Lotus 1-2-3	Poetry by Dr. Priser	Dad being diagnosed with multiple sclerosis
Milk and graham crackers late at night with Dad	Feeling all tingly listening to amazing classical music	Getting a B in chemistry
Chamber band trips	Totino's frozen pizza for Thanksgiving	Leadership roles – principal clarinet, yearbook editor-in-chief
Choosing NIU even though none of my friends were there	NIU Honors Program	Working in different areas at Richardson
The smell of freshly mown hay	Being alone and being a little fish in a big pond at NIU	Taking a chance on a scholarship to university in CA

Take that sheet and cut into pieces for each of the items. You should see some patterns emerging, so take the items and put them in different piles that seem to go together.

Using those piles as a starting point, create a list of 5-10 things that you think might be life success factors based on the things you are passionate about and your deepest held fears.

Using my examples above, I might have grouped the following together to form my life success factor of "Opportunities for active exploration:"

- Sports with my brothers at the bus stop
- Choosing books on topics about which I knew nothing
- Lotus 1-2-3
- Choosing NIU even though none of my friends were there
- Working in different areas at Richardson
- Taking a chance on a scholarship to university in CA

Hold on to this first draft of your life success factors as we will come back to them again in the next chapter and continue to refine them.

When I look back at how I wound up being a business major going to university on a music scholarship, it actually kind of makes sense when I look at my life success factors. No, it didn't address all six of them, but it did address my fear about finding a career that would put me somewhere above "upper lower class," and provide an entry into a career where there was a lot to learn, while exploring an entirely different part of the country.

We'll look next at how to use your life success factors to seize opportunities.

Chapter 3 – Using Your Life Success Factors to Create Opportunities

"There are myriad potential destinations. It is your choice of those destinations that is unique."

AS I APPROACHED THE END of undergrad, like everyone else, I had to start thinking about what was next for me. I had enjoyed my time in Southern California, but it wasn't the right fit for me, and I was ready to head back to the Midwest. As an accounting major, I wanted to obtain my CPA (Certified Public Accountant) license, which required not only passing a daunting multiple-day exam, but also a certain number of years of experience in a public accounting firm. Like many of my classmates, I dreamed of working for one of the then Big 6 professional services firms (in alphabetical order, Arthur Andersen, Coopers & Lybrand, Deloitte & Touche, Ernst & Young, KPMG, and Price Waterhouse). They were the behemoths that audited the largest companies in the world as well as provided tax and consulting services. I had a particular soft spot for Andersen, since their world training center was in St. Charles, Illinois, just about 15 minutes from where I grew up, and their world headquarters were in Chicago, so they had always loomed large in my mind.

I was, of course, just one of many thousands of accounting graduates each year who wanted to work for the Big 6. The firms had the luxury of being very selective and targeted in their recruiting and tended to shop at large universities with established accounting programs and high CPA exam pass rates. Yeah, well, my university was not on their radar due to its small size, though it actually had a 100 percent CPA exam pass rate the year I transferred there. Okay, only three students sat for the exam that year, but 100 percent is 100 percent!

In the last quarter of my junior year, I took my first tax class. And LOVED it. Who knew?! Tax is a very specialized area, with people who are serious about tax often either getting a Master of Taxation degree or, for the really crazy ones with a bizarre love for school and more debt, a law degree. And who'd want to spend three more years in school to get a law degree? (Oh, the irony....) As it so happened, Northern Illinois University, where I had attended university my first year, happened to have one of the top 10 accounting programs in the nation. Not only did it have a great CPA exam pass rate (and a much vaunted CPA review program), but one of its professors, Don Kieso, was the co-author of THE textbook for real accountants -- *Intermediate Accounting*, by Kieso & Weygant.[9] So my plan was to apply for the Masters in Tax program at NIU and then be in perfect position for recruitment by a Big 6 firm because NIU was most assuredly squarely in their recruitment sights. I applied, was accepted and even received a graduate research assistantship to help with costs. Terrific. All sorted out.

---

[9] *I still had my copy of this probably 3-inch thick tome at least 15 years after graduating as I couldn't bear to part with it even though it was outdated – it's that much of a thing. Also makes an excellent doorstop and is helpful in pressing leaves and flowers – so versatile!*

And then, in the first quarter of my senior year, I took my second tax class. And HATED it. *Ruh roh.* It was almost like high school chemistry all over again (though I think I got an A this time). So, was this class just an outlier? Or would I despise all other tax classes? Hard to know. And I was now two quarters from graduating. Since I had the master's program all lined up, I had stopped interviewing for potential jobs. I could take the somewhat safe route and proceed with the master's program and just drift along, but at the potential expense of winding up with a job and career in a field that I might not like. It seemed easy. And safe. But...

I took a closer look at the program and catalog for the master's program (unfortunately, it was still before all this type of information was available on a web site), trying to see if there was a way to possibly reduce the potential for unhappiness based on the electives I could take within the program. Maybe.

But I took another step back and saw that there were other Master in Accounting degrees beyond tax. One of them was with an Emphasis in Accounting Information Systems – fun, core accounting courses like advanced auditing theory coupled with information systems offerings like systems analysis and design, database management and telecommunications. A super geek degree. Recall how enthralled I was with learning Lotus 1-2-3 way back in high school? I hadn't lost my passion for technology and had actually taken a few programming classes in undergraduate (COBOL and Pascal, anyone?), but didn't have enough bandwidth to pursue a minor in it with my music commitments.

This was perfect!

So, I sent NIU a letter (it was the early '90s, recall) and respectfully requested admittance to the Master of Accounting Science program instead of the Master of Taxation and, um, any chance I might still be able to have a graduate research assistantship? They were gracious enough to both allow me to switch programs and to retain the assistantship. All the stars had aligned, and I was headed back to Illinois.

For my assistantship, I was assigned to a young assistant professor, Doug, who was focused on accounting information systems. I performed some research for him, graded papers and exams for his undergraduate courses, and also assisted with those courses. He was also very generous with his time and advice as I moved through the program.[10]

The program generally lasted about 18 months. If you really hustled and took classes over the summer, you could get it done in 12 months. But an advantage of going the longer route was the potential to do an internship (with academic credit) over the summer, with the hope that it would result in an offer of permanent employment after graduation. So, I started looking into internship opportunities through the Department of Accountancy's program. The program essentially provided ranking and matchmaking between employers and students that would result in a slate of interviews that may or may not lead to something that was a good fit. I realized the latter part as I started having

---

[10] *Doug received his PhD from the University of Wisconsin. Guess who was his dissertation chair? Jerry Weygandt, the other co-author of the infamous Kieso & Weygandt Intermediate Accounting. Small world, no?*

interviews for some of the internships. The companies were interesting, but I couldn't get a good sense for what I would actually be doing and whether it would be "real" work versus just some kind of busywork. I really wanted to apply what I'd been learning as well as learn more about the respective company and/or industry so I could get a better idea of what I might want to do later, whether I got a job offer or not (though that was certainly appealing for someone with a need for financial security).

By this point, I had quite a bit of experience working in a professional business setting. Every summer and sometimes over winter breaks during undergrad, I had returned to work for Richardson. I was a good worker and they were kind enough to always find a place for me. Kathy, their Vice President of Marketing Operations, was both respected and feared, but I got along with her really well. Whether by design or just due to current needs, each summer she slotted me in a different department. So, by the time I was in graduate school interviewing for internships, I already had experience in customer returns, purchasing, warehouse operations, customer service, marketing and advertising. I also had mad wicked skills with the copy machine. This experience allowed me to clearly see how all of the things I was learning in books translated into the real business world, which I think was a huge advantage and a gift for which I am still thankful. It also made me want to avoid a fluff internship because I didn't need to be taught how business works and didn't want to waste time on that.

So when I was in interviews for internships and the interviewer asked if I had any questions, they tended to be a bit taken aback when I started asking about supply chain optimization, whether they were using any Japanese methods for production, whether they were still using mainframes or had started to use mini-computers like the AS/400 (still one of my favorites), et cetera. One woman literally tipped her head to the side as I started asking these questions.

Too much? Oops.

I tried to learn how to rein myself in and just play eager for a job, but it wasn't authentic. I wanted to know what I was really in for and didn't feel like I was making progress or the kinds of connections that would lead to a meaningful internship.

So, I spoke with Doug and he asked if I had thought about an internship in IT audit. One of the things I had been learning through the master's program was that with the increasing use of technology, the types of internal controls over financial reporting that were previously performed by people, were not being built into and carried out by the accounting programs that companies used. As a result, it was becoming increasingly necessary for auditors to understand accounting information systems in order to conduct an efficient and effective audit. This was an area that I really wanted to focus on but, as I told Doug, there weren't any internship positions for IT audit.

And he responded with one of the most important questions for me for that moment and for life. "Why does it have to exist? Wouldn't it be a better fit if you defined it yourself?"

Ummm…. Yeah, but I can't hire myself.

He explained that if this was something I was interested in, then I needed to create a business case and sell it to one or more of the Big 6 accounting firms and convince them that while they didn't offer an IT audit at the time, they should offer one and they should pilot the idea by hiring me. It was bold. But I knew where I wanted to go. I just needed a channel to focus my energy. But this was *really* uncomfortable for me. After all, one of the reasons I wanted to be an accountant was that I didn't want to have to "sell" anything because I'm a bookish introvert.

I still marvel at Doug's generosity in not only helping me work through this idea, but also using his contacts to make introductions so I could pitch the idea to individuals who might be open to the concept. One of those individuals was Connie, another professor. Connie's area of teaching was not accounting information systems, but she agreed that it was a critical emerging area and something that the Big 6 should be considering. She had worked at Price Waterhouse and had a friend who was a leader in their Chicago recruiting team. She reached out to him and made the introduction. At the same time, Doug reached out to a classmate from his undergraduate days who happened to be a senior manager in the IT audit group of Ernst & Young and also made an introduction. And somehow, likely also through Doug, I received an introduction to a recruiter at Arthur Andersen.

Connections Matter

Where there was a personal connection to the firms with the introduction – former colleague, former classmate – it really mattered. I don't think that it was coincidence that the two firms that gave me an interview were the ones where I had a warm introduction. That didn't mean that I would necessarily get a position, or that they could even figure out how to create that position for me, but it certainly helped.

Not having a connection doesn't mean that you can't achieve great things through cold contacts, but a warm contact really helps. Because we know our friends and choose them carefully, we pay attention to what they say and are more open to ideas or, in this case, individuals they introduce. Of course, once you are in a position to leverage your contacts, it is important to pay it forward for others.

This was really amazingly exciting to me. And also, incredibly intimidating. Because we were operating outside of the normal internship/recruitment process, I couldn't just drift along with the process; I had to chart my own path. It was all on me. I had confidence in my abilities based on my course work and previous work experience, but I was not nearly so confident in the recruitment dance or interviews themselves. I'd been reading about effective interviewing techniques since I was a kid reading *Working Woman*, but that's different than actually being in the hot seat for an interview. I'd only had a few interviews in undergrad and the awkward ones in graduate school that I was now escaping. When you do an end run around a process, you may not know what you're actually running into.

Add to that, I had very little confidence and a lot of anxiety about how I dressed and looked. (And I still do today.) My self-confidence fortunately wasn't about whether I was ugly; I was fine with my physical features. But I grew up as a tomboy and had never really gone through the make-up phase and still didn't enjoy wearing skirts and heels. But I wasn't too proud to ask for help. When I was in undergrad, I went to the Marshall Field's[11] make-up counter and laid myself at their mercy, asking if they could help me learn how to do my make-up. The Estee Lauder ladies took pity on me and gave me a brief introduction, for which I am forever thankful. So I had a base level knowledge, but would never be taken for glamorous. I had also gone to Casual Corner, which seemed the best store for decent women's skirted suits and had bought a few of those. But there's a difference between having the clothes and being able to rock the look. It should surprise no one, then, that style is nowhere on my life success factors list. Yes, it's important to present yourself in a professional manner, but it's not something that is core to my values or something that I'm going to spend a lot of time worrying about. To be clear, I wasn't a slob. I was neat, tidy and paid attention to my appearance, but that's a world away from saying I had a sense of style or fashion.

Why this diversion into attire and make-up? Because the Big 6 firms were seen as the elite firms, with everyone

---

[11] *Marshall Field's was a department store with its flagship store on State Street in Chicago. It was acquired by Macy's in 2005, but I still have a difficult time referring to that particular location as anything other than Marshall Field's. Should you ever be in Chicago, it's worth a visit for lunch in the Walnut Room and to see both the gorgeous Tiffany ceiling and the classic clocks on the exterior. The building is a National Historic Landmark.*

being properly turned out and having a certain "look" and I was not at all sure that I would be able to fit in. I was particularly concerned about Arthur Andersen and Price Waterhouse. There was definitely an Andersen look and a certain element of prestige to be able to walk through their iconic double doors. And Price Waterhouse had the reputation of being the auditor's auditor, very white-shoe and the most conservative of the firms. I didn't really know enough about Ernst & Young to have specific concerns about it, but assumed it was similar to the others.[12]

It was one thing to be able to work my way in to interviews via an alternate route, but if I didn't have that look, would that limit me? Or put another way, despite the success I'd had so far, I was doubting whether a tomboy farm girl from modest means had any business or right to be interviewing with these prestigious firms. It makes me angry as I write that now because the resounding answer is, "Of course I did!" but it was nevertheless one of the thoughts lurking in the back of my head as I went through this process.

But as they say, nothing ventured, nothing gained. So, I put myself out there, took a bit of risk and moved forward. Ultimately, Arthur Andersen said that while they liked the idea, they didn't have time to get together a specific internship like this for the following summer. They did ask if I would check back in with them in the fall. I was successful

---

[12] *Perhaps this isn't entirely true, as Ernst & Young had been the auditors of Richardson when I worked there. Each year the coming of the auditors added a bit of interest to our otherwise calm lives and they were always pointed out in the company cafeteria.*

in obtaining interviews with both Price Waterhouse and Ernst & Young.

Choices are Always Accompanied by Risk

There are often multiple risks in any situation where choices are involved. Often, we say we're taking risks by doing something with a downside. Taking yourself out of your comfort zone. And yes, I suppose that is a risk. But we often don't take the time to think of the risk of inaction. Of staying in that comfort zone. Of drifting along. In the internship situation, I could have just continued with the awkward interviews in the established internship process and possibly scored an internship that would have been either a total waste of time or that could have led to a job offering. But in none of the instances would I have been pursuing the type of job that I ultimately wanted. An area that I believed would be important moving forward. A topic that combined the geeky things about which I was (and continue to be) passionate. So yes, doing what you love can represent some risk. But so can doing what you don't love.

One of the advantages of going outside of the traditional interview process was that I ended up entirely skipping the on-campus interviews that were essentially a way of weeding out candidates who may have looked good on paper but in person failed to measure up. But an interview is an interview and stressing in its own way, so I was happy to bypass that. I suppose the logic by the firms was that since I already had contacts via Doug and Connie who were known and respected, their recommendations eliminated the need for the on-campus screening interview.

An in-office interview is normally then where you have a good chance of landing an internship, so you just have to make sure you don't screw up. Although in my case, I felt like I still needed to "sell" the idea since it was something that both of these firms would be creating just for me. And because it was new, they might also still be mulling through whether indeed they wanted to create something like that and, if so, what it should look like. So, I was still nervous.

The Price Waterhouse interview was first. I checked in with the receptionist on the 75th or so floor of the Amoco Building (now the Aon Center) and was treated to gorgeous views of Lake Michigan through their large glass windows while I waited for someone to fetch me. It was impressive. And eerily quiet. But I could imagine myself working there and seeing that view every day.

At the time, none of the firms recruited even full-time college graduates directly into their IT audit groups. The practices were small and targeted in their work. So, they recruited internally from their audit ranks from seniors with three or more years of auditing work who exhibited some interest or skill related to IT. Since the firms didn't have entry level IT audit positions, it made sense, then, that they wouldn't have had a need for internship positions that would then feed into entry level hires.

Normally, when firms bring in candidates for office visits, they assigned someone at the level for which the individuals were interviewing to be a sort of host or coordinator to not only welcome the candidates, but escort them to various offices for interviews, take them to lunch, and answer general questions. Be a buddy for the day and give them a sense of what a "day in the life" looks like. But since my position didn't exist, there weren't people who would be in my peer group to serve as hosts.

So, I had a manager as a host – someone with at least five years of experience versus one or two that might be normal for an intern candidate. I had a lovely time. I interviewed with several senior managers and a partner, had a somewhat informal lunch with the hosting manager, and came away with a good sense of the job and feeling about Price Waterhouse, but also an offer in hand. Woohoo!!! And also, a handsome navy portfolio embossed with the Price Waterhouse logo (the one that existed prior to their 1998 merger with Coopers & Lybrand).

My first reaction was to accept the offer immediately. I mean, what if they changed their mind? But I also knew it would be incredibly rude to not proceed with the interview with Ernst & Young, especially after Doug had gone out of his way to make an introduction for me.

The Ernst & Young offices were in the Sears Tower (now Willis Center), the tallest building in the world at that time, though their offices were at lower levels and the views weren't nearly as nice as those at Price Waterhouse. From the start, though, I sensed a totally different vibe than at Price Waterhouse. For starters, Ernst & Young had been formed several years before through the combination of Ernst & Whinney and Arthur Young, and their space at the Sears Tower was the first office in Chicago for the combined firm. They had implemented a new type of office facilities approach called hoteling. For staff and seniors, you were assigned a file cabinet and drawers and when you were actually in the office, you made a reservation for a workspace for that day or week and took the things you needed from your file cabinet to your desk and put them back when your reservation ended. This made sense, particularly for auditors who were often at client locations, so it was silly (and expensive) to leave workspaces empty for the majority of the time. Managers, senior managers and partners, however, had offices.

The other thing that was quickly obvious to me on the day of my interview was that I was significantly overdressed. Unbeknownst to me, that particular day was the first ever "casual Friday" at the office. Because it was so new, no one had thought to tell me about this. So while everyone was trying to figure out what was allowed as business casual attire, I rolled in with my conservative navy suit and sensible pumps. Um, er… And almost everyone seemed to apologize about their business casual attire, noting it was the first day, they weren't sure what to wear, etc.… In retrospect, I'm glad that I didn't know as I would have been even more stressed out about what to wear!

My host for the day was Dave, a relatively new senior in the group who still worked on audits during busy season in addition to IT audit work. He took me to my first interview, the classmate of Doug's who was a senior manager in the group. She set me at ease before lunch with Dave and another colleague. The lunch was, er…, interesting. I expected it to be something like the lunch at Price Waterhouse – nice, but still somewhat casual. Apparently, that was the idea, but it didn't quite turn out that way.

The Metropolitan Club is a members' only club located on the 66th and 67th floors of the Sears Tower. We were to have lunch in the relatively casual location that had an upscale version of a buffet and may have also had items you could order from a menu. Except that that location was closed for remodeling, so we were taken to the formal dining room. And I do mean formal. This is more what I had in mind when they mentioned it was a members' only club. Quiet, beautiful lake views and with excellent, attentive staff. A place where a farm girl did not feel very comfortable, even for someone who *had* read Emily Post's book on etiquette to learn which fork and knife to use (thank goodness for my random library selections!).

I felt slightly better because Dave and his colleague seemed somewhat confused by the situation as well as they were not themselves club members but were the guests of a partner who was probably more familiar with this type of environment. I don't know what I ordered for an entrée, but distinctly recall that I ordered a soup to start. The solicitous server – literally with a white towel hanging perfectly from his tucked arm – presented the bowl to me and said something that I didn't quite catch because I was staring at the contents. There were a series of vegetables and herbs arranged in a sort of hash pattern. Just sitting in an empty bowl.

Um, am I missing something here? I'm pretty sure I ordered a soup. Does soup for fancy people not come in liquid form?

As luck would have it, of course, I was the only one who had ordered the, er, "soup." The guys were looking at me. Stalling, I asked, "Oh, what did you order for a starter?"

Right around that time, servers delivered their starters and with a fancy vessel began pouring broth over the vegetable/herb artistic arrangement in my bowl, gently so as not to splash the broth, and which gently brought said vegetables and herbs floating to the surface while maintaining the hash pattern. Magical. I almost didn't want to slurp it up. But I did. (I mean, I had the soup, but I did not slurp – give me a little credit for recall on what I'd read in Emily Post.)

And I got my second internship offer, so I must have done okay.

Chapter 4 – The Link Between Authenticity and Life Success Factors

*"You can't be centered in life if you don't know
who you are and where you want to be."*

WITH TWO INTERNSHIP OFFERS in hand, I had to choose. They were both great firms. I liked the people at both. The compensation was nearly identical. The work would likely be the same. Other than one having spectacular views of Lake Michigan and the other allowing business casual on Friday, there didn't seem to be a lot of difference. I was confident I would have a great experience and be happy at either firm. So how to choose?

One of the people I interviewed with at EY was a senior manager named Bill. And he laughed. Openly. Frequently. Not at me, of course, but at things he found funny. At life. At stories he told. At things his kids did, who were clearly the focus of his life. He was full of joy and not worried about that slipping out.

I also interviewed with the partner leading the practice, Trish. Not surprisingly, she asked a lot of questions from a business perspective about why I thought an internship would be a good idea for them since they didn't even hire staff directly.

Because there aren't that many individuals with a combination of technology and accounting knowledge, so the sooner you can identify them, the better your pipeline of qualified candidates. And you can likely improve engagement economics by leveraging some tasks to lower-cost resources. And you can try this out with me with no recruiting costs involved since I came with the idea to you and I'm even less expensive than a staff resource.

Nothing speaks louder to a partner than engagement economics and winning the war for talent, even back then. We had a good conversation and I think I convinced her that it was at least worth a shot. What impressed me more, though, was that she started out with a somewhat apologetic self-disclosure that she'd been uncertain about what to wear that day because it was the first day of business casual and she wasn't sure what that meant for women in business and she apologized (to me!) if she was dressed too casual.

Yeah, I'm actually here as a supplicant to beg for an internship. You owe me zero apologies. And you also look fine to a tomboy who knows nothing about fashion, let alone business casual. (She was wearing what I now recognize as a St. John knit suit, though perhaps it was the color -- red with white stripes – that concerned her about it being too casual?)

Maybe she appreciated that, since I hadn't gotten the memo about it being business casual Friday and had shown up in my navy suit, I felt a bit out of place. But I took it as her being authentic and even a bit vulnerable.

You can see where this is going. I accepted the internship offer from EY because I felt a bit more comfortable that I would be able to be myself and authentic from the first day. And while it's certainly possible that I had given those two interactions during my interviews much more credence than was deserved, the months and years that followed reinforced that they were accurate about the character and culture not only of Bill and Trish, but of the firm overall.

It's not enough to have identified your life success factors if you don't put yourself in places where you can openly and actively pursue them.

Authenticity and Covering

If you're not independently wealthy, you'll will spend much of your days and life at work, so finding a job where you are happy can have a significant impact on your happiness in life. And you'll be happier at a job where you can genuinely be yourself.

There is real science behind being authentic and the energy we waste not being so and hiding a part of ourselves: "covering."

Much of the research, books and articles about covering relate to certain characteristics of individuals where there is a perceived bias against those traits, such that disclosing them or not trying to fit in could be detrimental to one's career. I first heard of it in the context of LGBTQ individuals who refer to their significant other by a different gender. (Kenji Yoshino's book, Covering, *is a nice read, walking through literature on covering as well as his own experience with covering through his life as a man who is both gay and Asian.) There are many other examples of covering, such as women in a predominantly male profession trying to act like the guys, downplaying nationality or ethnicity when you are a minority, suppressing how important your religion or belief system may be, etc. But we can also cover by just holding back.*

To not let your quirks show. To keep a part of you hidden. To not let your friends know that you secretly enjoy splitting wood. That you named your cats after the Sarbanes-Oxley Act of 2002. That you struggle with the shame of owning a John Deere tractor when your family taught you that International Harvester (now Case International, alas) is superior. That you write poems about your car. Those are just a few weird things about me that I probably will not tell you as soon as I meet you because you may likely think I'm off my rocker. And you might be right. Or you might be missing out on a potential connection point. You won't know which is correct, though, unless I am comfortable enough to introduce those topics. This is why finding a job where I felt at ease being all of those things was really important to me.

So, I accepted the offer. I had a great time during the internship and they offered me a permanent position after I graduated, which I readily accepted.[13] By the time I joined full-time, Bill had been promoted to partner and we all knew when he was in the office because we could hear his booming laughter warming the halls, reminding me why I had chosen the firm.

I joined in January, which was the beginning of audit busy season during which the audit teams were focused on the financials of companies with fiscal years ending December 31. The audit teams worked insane hours from January through at least March. With the advent of IT audit, we could use computers to perform some of the tasks that previously had to be performed by pencil and paper, taking a little bit of pressure off the teams. And to the extent that our audit clients were relying on computers and related system controls, we had to understand and test those as well, which was the responsibility of our team.[14]

---

[13] *When I was pitching the idea of the internship, Arthur Andersen had noted that they didn't have time to put an internship together before the upcoming summer, but they'd be interested in speaking with me afterwards. So I did follow up with them. I remember being at a lunch (somewhere between the casual Price Waterhouse lunch and the fancy floating herb and veggie soup of EY) with two professionals from Andersen and realizing I kept saying "we" when discussing EY, so apparently the firm's brainwashing of me during the internship was successful!*

[14] *I realize "system controls" is not a standard vocabulary term for those who are not accountants. In case you may have some interest, let me try to put it in context with the example of buying something online. As you check out, you see the price of each item, the quantity you want to buy of each, applicable sales tax, if any, as well as shipping charges, and perhaps a discount code. The system controls ensure*

Audit teams are highly structured as a certain level of experience is required to work through more complex accounts and procedures. Junior staff[15] might work on cash and accounts receivable which are pretty straightforward, whereas senior managers would work on more complicated areas that involved considerable judgment or technical knowledge. Depending on the size of the company being audited, the team could be in the field for quite a long period of time, even though they worked long hours. The partner and senior managers might have multiple audits going on at the same time and would visit the respective client sites, but the staff and seniors were there pretty much every day.

IT controls was one of the areas requiring some additional expertise that was applied in a relatively short period of time in the field for each audit but involved juggling

---

that the price listed is the price charged, that it applies the correct sales tax for the state in question, that the discount is applied before the sales tax is calculated, etc. In a nutshell, they make sure that you're charged the right amount for what you ordered, that the company collects (and later remits) the right amount of sales tax, and that the sale is accurately recorded as sales revenue, et cetera, on the appropriate date in the company's accounting records. Ages ago, this would have been done manually, later with the aid of a calculator, and now almost seamlessly in the background. So auditors double-check that the formulae are working as designed, that there are limits on who can change the formulae, and that the right revenue, costs and expenses are reported in the financial statements on which investors rely. It may sound a bit boring, but it's important in the efficient operation of our capital markets.

[15] *The hierarchy and career progression of most professional accounting firms is generally a couple years as a staff, a few more as a senior during which you begin supervising others, then manager for yet more years, then to senior manager where you spend a number of years until you are ready to be promoted to an equity partner or similar non-equity position or get the gentle hint that such a promotion will not be forthcoming.*

multiple clients that needed certain procedures to be performed. The professionals carrying out these duties were part of a specialized team and were, at a minimum, seniors. Well, at least until I came along. Since I had already taken the IT controls training during my internship that most only received when they were seniors, when I showed up at an audit client, the rest of the audit team just assumed I was a senior. I admit that I did nothing to disabuse them of this notion, though I didn't lie about my level when asked (and this was long before we had an intranet where people could look up the levels of professionals). I just kept my head down, did my work and tried to figure out what, exactly, that was! Later in the year when I started to actually do audits as a staff, it really made me chafe at being so restricted and not manage where and when I would be at clients' sites!

One of my favorite parts of the work was testing physical security over IT assets, which inevitably led to the Chief Information Officer or Chief Technology Officer walking me through his[16] "glass house."[17] While I did need to know some information, it was a great opportunity to talk with technology leaders and hear what was on their minds. And they were always eager to talk shop (and often – the stereotype is somewhat true – Star Trek). Questions I posed about how they decided to choose a particular server or to migrate from a mainframe to an AS/400 or minicomputer

---

[16] *Sadly, at the time, they were all men. I hope that is different today.*

[17] *Most of the data centers at the time were behind a wall of glass, hence "glass house." I have no idea why that was, other than to be able to walk by it and see a bunch of lights flashing, maybe hear a faint whirring?*

were met with as much enthusiasm as asking a parent if they might have photos of their children. Most of the communication was one-way with me asking a lot of questions, but the more settled I became in the position, the more I started fielding questions from them about what I was seeing in other shops and my opinions on some technology. I carefully avoided the latter because our job was to audit, but I was happy to share with them what I was generally seeing across my variety of clients.

What I learned from this (in addition to the technology information, of course) was the importance of asking good questions, and the right types of questions to elicit the information I needed. You know by now that opportunities for active exploration is one of my life success factors, so it won't surprise you that asking questions and hearing the answers fed into my need to know more. But it was, and is, more than that.

Questions build relationships. We humans are largely egocentric. We like to hear ourselves talk. We like to know (or at least think) that others value what we think. Advice to that effect goes as far back as Dale Carnegie's, *How to Make Friends and Influence People*, which was published in 1936, but is just as true today and worth the read. Studies have also shown that people think you are more interesting when, in an initial conversation, you've asked questions and they've pretty much done all the talking. We are apparently just wired like that.

Questions were also lifesavers for me at the time because at times I felt a bit intimidated by the CIO or CTO. Here I was, a young professional hardly out of college asking someone who is decades older than me and at the top of his game. Having the right questions actually credentialed me indirectly to show him that I knew what I was talking about but was smart enough to want to learn from his experience. Once I got him talking, it was much easier for me to relax.

So, whether active exploration is one of your life success factors or not, it pays to think about questions. It helps to draw out people, builds and strengthens relationships, expands your own knowledge and, quite frankly, allows another person to fill up spaces where you're not sure what to say yourself. If you know in advance that you're going to meet someone who's, say, an astrophysicist, it might be daunting to think of what to say to her since the great majority of us have no clue what that entails. But there's the opportunity. By asking open-ended questions, you can actually learn what astrophysics is all about.

- *How did you first become interested in astrophysics?*
- *How did you set about learning about it?*
- *How did you choose that university over others?*
- *What do you think is the most interesting part of astrophysics that most of us may not know?*
- *How, if at all, does the field have an impact on the day-to-lives of all of us?*

You get the idea. I highly recommend getting in the habit of thinking up questions you want to pose. When I was in graduate school, an NIU accounting alumnus who was a partner from a Big 6 accounting firm was slated to address an assembly of several hundred accounting and business students. Beforehand, Doug asked if I was going to ask any questions. I responded that, well, I didn't know because I didn't know what he was going to say. I'll never forget what he said. "The purpose of questions isn't always to interrogate others about what they want to talk about, but to interrogate your own knowledge and understanding and try to fill in gaps with information and experience that others have already gathered."

Oh. Noted. I did ask a question that day (something about how he managed to keep up on both general business developments, accounting developments and the regulatory environment when so much information was coming out all the time – oh, the irony, as this was well before the explosion of information on the Internet, so it'd still be a decent question today). I was nervous doing so in front of all of those other students and with a Big 6 accounting firm partner (I realized later that they're actually normal people, too). Heart pounding, voice threatening to quaver. But I did it. After all, I'd likely never see the guy again, so what did I have to lose? But I realized later that it was a decent question, I'd gotten an answer on how to focus my reading in a professional environment and had taken advantage of an opportunity while others had just sat glued in their seats, staring at the guy.

I'm belaboring the importance of questions because asking questions is fundamental to identifying opportunities that may be consistent with your life success factors. And questions are also key to creating relationships with others who can exponentially increase the number and types of opportunities to which you may have access.

I feel compelled to offer two cautions on questions. First, we all have been annoyed by the person who wastes our time asking questions to ingratiate himself with the professor, boss or other person of some esteem or power. As in everything, moderation is key.

Second, be judicious when asking for action versus asking for information. Action requires a lot more commitment (and usually time) from the other person. While it never hurts to ask a question, you'll inevitably arrive at a better result if you earn the right to ask the question by first earning a bit of trust from the other individual and showing respect for her, her time and her responsibilities.

Time is one of the most valuable resources we have because it's so limited. And, Economics 101, the more limited the resource, the higher the price. Approaching someone who is a virtual stranger and asking for her to take action on your behalf is more or less like asking her to give you some money just because you ask for it. Yes, people will give money to strangers, but there's usually some kind of exchange even there – we want to help that person who may or may not actually be homeless get a train ticket home, or we want to help save the children or rainforests or we believe that we're paying it forward or whatever. But the bigger the ask, the bigger the implicit exchange.

I was making a big ask out of the three firms when I asked them to consider offering an internship to me that they'd never offered to anyone. I wanted them to go outside of their well-oiled recruiting and internship process, use the limited time of their professionals to come up with a program (when those same resources normally would be generating revenue for the firm), and to use even more resources to pay me to work for them as an intern. That's a pretty big ask. So, I didn't just say, "Can you give me an internship, please?" Instead, I crafted a business case and highlighted the potential benefits to them of offering such an internship and demonstrated my own ability to contribute by having brought this opportunity to them. I allowed them to try before they bought, in a certain sense. They certainly could have still said no, but I tried to make it as easy as possible for them to say yes and, fortunately for me, they were receptive.

A similar example is that of mentoring. We have all heard of the importance of mentors in our lives, but less time is spent on how one actually obtains mentors. Or as I like to say, "recruit" mentors, because it should be an active, deliberate process in which both parties benefit. Real mentoring takes time and isn't a one-off exchange.

No matter how much you may admire someone (and perhaps *particularly* if you really admire someone), don't introduce the mentoring topic without laying the foundation. Not too long ago, I had just given a speech at an event to a large group of professionals within our firm. A young woman approached me as I left the stage, introduced herself (just her name and her practice) and asked if I would be her mentor. Um, what? I was a total deer in the headlights. While I give her credit for being bold and making the ask, I didn't even know her. I had no idea why she would want me as her mentor and it put me in a realllllly awkward position (specifically, wanting to run or hide).

I am by no means suggesting you should never formally ask someone to mentor you, but unless you work with an organization that has a formal mentoring program, I think it's much more effective to let mentor/mentee relationships just grow spontaneously. You meet someone. You find out a little bit about her and her areas of interest. You identify some potential commonalities and, hopefully, some key differences (because you want to seek out a different perspective than yours). You start by thinking of how you can help her. And *then* think about how she might be able to assist you.

Somewhere around my third year with the firm, we hired a gentleman into the practice at the senior manager level (two levels and many more years of experience ahead of me). Jay had a lot of experience in the insurance industry, was charismatic and fun, but he knew nothing about the day-to-day operations of an accounting firm. So as odd as it sounds given the disparity in our positions, I took him under my wing. I volunteered to help him learn how to do small things like time sheets or open new engagement codes – things that weren't complicated, but that I knew how to do and he didn't, and that might have felt awkward for someone at his level to ask about. This then turned into discussions about engagements and clients. And I started asking (yes, lots of questions) for his opinion on how to deal with difficult colleagues and client personnel, what he had experienced working in industry and whether he needed help with any projects. And he became a mentor.

Neither of us identified our relationship as mentor/mentee, but that's exactly what it was. For many years, he became my go-to person on business development and client relationship management. I had other mentors for other topics (my personal board of directors, as some call it), but that area was his sweet spot, so a perfect mentoring area. But I started out by asking how I could help him; I was interested in **his** success. Not because I thought he might be a mentor, but because he was a colleague and I genuinely wanted him to succeed. We developed a relationship and it became natural for him to want to help me right back.

I've been incredibly fortunate to have found mentors throughout my career and life and all have arisen in very different ways. But when I think of every single one that has become a lifetime relationship, many of which have also developed into close personal friendships, it started out with me trying to help them. There are probably other ways of developing successful mentoring relationships, but this is what has worked for me.

Mentors are opportunity scouts. When they truly know who you are, what you're capable of, what's important to you and what you're looking for, they will keep their eyes out for opportunities for you. They often operate in spheres of influence that you do not yet have, so they can spot (or create) opportunities before you are even aware of them.

My first audit busy season with the firm, I performed computer assisted audit tests (CAATS – meow), an elementary version of what would now be considered data analytics. Essentially, we would receive large data files from the mainframe computer or other systems of clients usually containing inventory and accounts receivable information. We pulled the data into an analytics program, queried the data and produced reports that the audit teams would then use in performing physical inventory counts and accounts receivable confirmations. I really enjoyed the work. It harkened back to my early days of programming as we wrote the scripts, debugged them, and tried to add in fancy features like histograms and other distributions. The more I played around with the software, the more I wondered whether there wasn't more that we could be doing with the data. Perhaps we could – [insert the *Law & Order* don-don sound here] – find fraud! I was gently reminded that that was not in the audit program, not our responsibility and, well, there wasn't enough time in the budget to do additional procedures that were not requested. [SIGH] But I kept bringing up the topic to anyone who would listen (ah, questions). Even if, perhaps, they didn't want to listen. I was the squeaky wheel.

Two years into my job, I was a bit bored. Because of the unusual way in which I had entered the ranks, I was doing the work as a staff professional that would normally have been performed by someone at the senior level with at least two more years of experience. So, when I was promoted to senior, I was promoted to, um, continue what I had already been doing for the past two years. Hence the boredom.

Around this time, I was assigned to a long-term project assisting a client with their implementation of SAP, an enterprise resource planning system, helping them convert their financial statement close process from their old system to the new system and teaching their accounting team how to implement the new process. This was actually kind of exciting because I was working closely with some really cool individuals at the client, SAP was cutting edge at the time[18] and it was my first project where we defined what we would be doing rather than simply executing on a pre-defined work program. Looking back, I see that it checked off opportunity for active exploration, teaching and creativity. But it was also more or less a 9-5 job, which I hadn't previously experienced in the firm where we usually worked 50-hour weeks during slow times and much more during busy season, so I suddenly had extra time in the evening. I'm not sure whether there is a mental or temporal version of "Idle hands are the devil's workshop," but that's kind of where I was.

I had started dating a guy right around the time I joined the firm full-time. He was older than me, having served in the Army Rangers for a while before getting his college degree, but we were both setting out into the business world around the same time. As the years wore on, he became disenchanted with his job and thought that perhaps he should get his MBA. So we headed to the bookstore so he could look for books to study for the GMAT (Graduate Management Admission Test). Well, I already had a master's degree so had no interest in GMAT books, so I started thumbing through books nearby including the MCAT and GRE books and – "Hello, what's this?!" – the LSAT books. Contents were more or less like this:

---

[18] *SAP is a German company. When we were assisting the client implementing SAP, it was such an early version that some of the instructions within the system were still in German. And, naturally, the abbreviated field names were also based on the German terms. When I lived in Germany years later, suddenly it all made a whole lot more sense.*

There are four people seated at a table. Tom is wearing a red sweater and is seated next to Patti, who is wearing corduroys. If Patti is next to Richard and only one person is wearing jeans, is it Sam who is wearing the plaid vest?

A. No. Sam is wearing a peach tunic.
B. Yes, but Sam is not the one wearing jeans.
C. Duh.
D. Not enough information to determine

Obviously, I made that all up, but it was nearly an entire book of puzzles. I was fascinated and compelled to buy the book for no apparent reason other than to amuse myself during those evenings of free time (even though the guy didn't buy the GMAT book or ever, as far as I know, take the GMAT test). The LSAT is, of course, the Law School Admission Test and your score on the test, combined with your undergraduate (but not graduate, oddly) GPA, had a significant impact on where and whether you might be accepted into a law school. Color me curious.

Once I had worked through the entire book (it was at least 2-3 inches thick, made of some great recycled kind of paper that smelled like a cross between wet newspaper and those awesome beige ruled and dotted papers of first grade), I took the practice test. And did pretty well.

Hmmmm….. Maybe I should sign up to take the test.

Why? Since when do you want to go to law school?

I don't. That's why I was initially pursuing a master's in tax rather than a law degree. Duh.

Well....?

Well, it's an opportunity and, just think, more puzzles sprung upon me in a time-controlled study![19]

Oh, okay, got it. Bring it!

So that's how I ended up taking the LSAT. Way back then, it took months to get your scores, by which time I was off of the 9-5 job and back to my regular job, but still a bit bored. Until a senior manager called me into her office and told me that our practice was creating a computer forensics group. Jay had mentioned that I was interested in fraud, so would this be something that might be of interest to me?

I have no idea what computer forensics is. But if Jay thought it might be something for me....

Did I mention that mentors can be opportunity scouts?

The guys (and they were all men) the firm had recruited to start the practice were primarily drawn from government, military and law enforcement. Not unlike Jay, they were new to the weird-to-them way the firm operated, so I tried to help as much as I could. And they began sharing their craft with me. Understanding not only logical file structures, but how a computer physically writes and overwrites to a hard drive. The breadcrumbs a deleted file leaves behind. How to get a sense of what happened on the computer by examining the hard drive. This was long before the *CSI* shows on TV, but it was just as compelling to me. Was it fraud investigation? No. But it was sooooo much sexier and more interesting than what I was otherwise doing. And, oh

---

[19] *I am one of those freaks of nature who enjoys multiple choice tests.*

yeah, opportunities for active exploration and creativity. Pinch me!

I had almost forgotten about the LSAT scores when they arrived. I plugged them into various calculators and determined that, with my undergrad GPA, I could probably get into some pretty decent law schools. But I still was definitely not convinced that I wanted to go to law school. I had a newly fascinating job with great colleagues, was nearly debt-free, and thought there were lots of opportunities ahead. Yet I was intrigued.

I did some research and, unfortunately, all the law schools in Chicago were private and thus quite expensive. I decided that if I did go to law school, I'd prefer to come out of the experience with something approaching a car payment rather than a mortgage payment so that I'd be free to practice whatever type of law I might want, rather than focused on what I'd need to pay off my loans. So, I applied to the University of Illinois, University of Wisconsin and University of Minnesota. And then I started getting acceptance letters.

So, this is for real?

Yeah.

I was ready for this new challenge. I ultimately settled on the University of Wisconsin. It has a unique approach to the law called Law in Action. The approach goes beyond merely teaching the rules and regulation of law, but also explores how and why those rules came to be and the practicalities of how those laws operate in the real world. In addition, my parents had moved near Madison, Wisconsin, while I was in undergraduate, so I would have some local support.

When I explained to my colleagues that I would be leaving the firm and the Chicago area to go to law school in Wisconsin, there were some blank stares. And then, "Why?" Not why was I going to law school, but why would I leave the firm? Why not transfer to the Milwaukee office and continue working via one of the new-at-the-time flexible work arrangements (FWAs)?

"But FWAs are only for women with children," I explained to these newbies to the firm. And then *they* schooled *me.* **They described** how FWAs were available for a variety of needs and the person wanting one just had to explain what they wanted, agree to a plan with her supervisor about the number of hours that would be worked, particular days of the week (if applicable), and work through any other potential barriers or considerations.

Really?

Yes, really. So I applied and did indeed receive a flexible work arrangement to attend law school full-time (UW Law did not have a part-time program), work a maximum of 20 hours when school was in session, work full-time during summer and other breaks, continue to enjoy the success and learning I was achieving at the firm and also keeping an income stream, albeit a reduced one.

When I look back on this now, I see that I created an environment when entering law school that maintained some of the life success factors that I had before, but I was realizing them through different means. For example, I was still enjoying learning and teaching at work, but now would obviously be adding quite a bit more learning. As an experienced law student, I had the opportunity to share with some of my classmates who were straight out of undergraduate about how businesses really worked. Through the flexible work arrangement, I was able to create some sense of financial stability in the short term, while also setting myself up for longer-term success in that factor with the addition of new, marketable skills following law school graduation.

It is really important to check in with your life, habits and how you spend your time and compare them against how (or whether) they align with your life success factors. Just because you're hitting a lot of your factors doesn't mean that you couldn't be doing other things that would hit the factors even more frequently. There is also a risk, too, of becoming complacent. The idea behind identifying your life success factors is not to pinpoint what makes you happy at one point in time. Rather, life success factors are guideposts that will help you gravitate towards growth opportunities related to what makes you happy and fulfilled in general, and that in turn will propel you towards your life vision.

This is where goals come in. Recall that goals are not the same as life success factors. The factors themselves generally don't change throughout your life, but your discrete goals certainly will.

Let's take, for example, my health life success factor and say that I have decided that running will be one way for me to improve my health. Except I don't currently run. So I set a goal of running a local 5K race in three months. I download an app that provides me with a training plan for how to be ready in three months. I put in the time doing the workouts. The race day comes, I run, and I finish the race.

Great. I've met the goal, right? And hopefully my health has improved as a result.

But what happens now? It's time to re-assess. It would be silly to set the same goal because I've already accomplished that goal. If I've fallen in love with running, perhaps I'd set a new goal to improve my time by a minute at another 5K. Or maybe I would realize that I am a slow-twitch muscle person, so longer distances may be better running goals and I may want to train towards a 10K. Or maybe I've learned that I don't really care for running, so I might try cycling. Or add in strength training to strengthen my leg muscles. Or take a class on healthy cooking.

Life often is not so organized, though, and you may need to re-assess mid-stream (or mid-goal) as opportunities arise. Let's say I'm working on that 5K goal. The training is going well, my level of fitness is improving and I'm touching on my health life success factor every time I lace up my shoes. But then I run into a friend who is starting a program to teach low income children how to play tennis to help improve not only their fitness, but to provide a safe and supportive environment for them. If part of my life vision is to give back and create a better world for our children, switching from my 5K goal to teaching tennis might very well make sense as I could still be active and working towards better health while also firing up my teaching life success factor.

We will talk about goals and habits in greater detail later on, but the important point is to periodically check in on your alignment with both your life success factors and whether you are growing.

On that note, make sure you are keeping an eye on *all* of your life success factors. The more factors you have, the more difficult this may be, so I recommend having no fewer than three but no more than seven. It's easier to track fewer factors but having more goals may create a broader basis for overall fulfillment rather than relying too much on a few areas. While I feel comfortable having six factors, I have made the mistake of losing sight of factors at times.

When I was considering the flexible work arrangement during law school, for example, I didn't realize that I was de-prioritizing my health. Going to school full-time at a competitive Tier 1[20] law school while working part-time and trying to still perform there at a high level and shuttling between Madison and Milwaukee really took a lot of time and energy and I didn't consciously make time to keep fit and healthy. When I applied to law school, the guy I was dating and I were very active through running, mountain biking, backpacking and other activities, and I took that for granted. I didn't stop and think at all about what I would be doing once I started law school to keep fit and healthy. If I had done so, I hope that I would have set out some sort of fitness plan or something so that I made time for working out. Unfortunately, I didn't, and my health has never been as good as it was before law school and I can't blame all of that merely on age. I also lost the habit of fitness being a natural part of my week and life. This was, admittedly, also before I had created my life success factors and once I did that, it has

---

[20] *The top 50 law schools in the US News law school rankings.*

been easier for me to make sure that I am taking time to make health a priority.

Monitoring is important in terms of alignment with your life success factors as well as in your overall growth. If you're not growing, then no matter how aligned your life may be with your life success factors, your energy will start dispersing rather than being properly channeled. You will not even realize that opportunities to create a better life in keeping with those life success factors are passing you by. Unexpected changes in circumstances (for example, sickness, death of a family member, natural disaster) may cause you to agree to grow at a slower rate for a period of time but be ever vigilant about maintaining forward momentum. Newton summarized it well:

> *"An object a rest stays at rest and an object in motion stays in motion with the same speed and at the same direction unless acted upon by an unbalanced force."*
>
> *~ Newton's First Law*

Monitoring alignment with your life success factors will help you manage your reactions to unbalanced forces and keep you moving in the right direction yet allowing for changes in course when they make sense for you.

Chapter 5 – The Perils of Forgetting You Have Multiple Life Success Factors

"The storms and elements of life expose who we are at our core."

LAW SCHOOL WAS NOT NEARLY as much fun as the LSAT puzzles. I remain mystified as to why the puzzles were (and perhaps still are) considered at all relevant to the study of law. I mean, I get that lawyers should have some sense of logic in order to put together compelling arguments, but the practice of law is much more about obtaining and understanding facts, perspectives and objectives and then applying the law to them. Several studies have shown that success in the practice of law, defined in varying ways, has pretty much zero correlation with LSAT scores. But nevertheless, my own scores and GPA had combined to take me where I was, enrolled in a competitive law school with a bunch of young, smart and motivated classmates.

I didn't find UW Law to be anything like some of the horrors you see in movies with some professors who were mean bordering on crazy combined with cutthroat competition from one's peers. Yes, some professors used the Socratic Method more than others, and every one of them were very demanding, but they were primarily focused on making sure that we understood the subject matter and were generous in their time to assist us when necessary.

But there was also a concerted effort by the administration to make the law firm faculty approachable. One such effort was the Faculty/1L (first year law student) reception. This was about a week into the term and was an opportunity for the newbies to get to know the professors and administration in a more casual setting, which included complimentary food and beverages. Recall that while I had been out in the working world for about five years by this point, most of my classmates were straight out of undergrad. So, there was a slight difference in my approach to the event versus some (though certainly not all) of my classmates.

Me: *Oh, a networking opportunity. I need to identify who I want to talk with and seek those individuals out to take full advantage of the gathering.* (Just as the firm had taught me.)
Classmates: *Dude! Free food and beer!!*

One of the individuals I wanted to meet was the dean of the law school itself. When I walked in, he was wide open, just chatting casually with the head of Development. I introduced myself, noting I was a manager at EY specializing in computer forensics and that I'd noticed that there was an Arthur Andersen room – what would we need to do to get a bigger, better room named after EY? (Yes, I really *was* that socially inept at the time.)

We had an interesting discussion about the law school, the Big 6 firms and my work. They were particularly interested in electronic discovery, electronic evidence and computer forensics since that was a very new field at the time, so I was happy to share my experience. I like to think I may have actually added some value.

At the end, though, the dean noted that our firm's general counsel was a UW Law graduate, and would I give her his regards? Sure, no problem. Now, at the time, I realized that the general counsel was our head lawyer for the firm, but not much else. And I also figured (possibly correctly) that unless I did something so grossly negligent that I single-handedly got the firm sued for multiple millions of dollars, I would never pop up on her radar. And given that I had no plans to do something negligent, I followed through and sent her an e-mail. There's a much longer story, but suffice it to say she was a much bigger deal both within the firm and in her career than I had imagined, having argued something like 14 cases before the U.S. Supreme Court, not to mention having been involved with some of the very cases that we ended up studying as 1Ls.

Even if I'd known that, I think I still would have sent the email. I strongly believe in the phrase, "nothing ventured, nothing gained." In a situation like this, I try to think: what's the worst that could go wrong, what's the best possible outcome, what's the likelihood of either scenario, and what is the worst potential impact on me?

In this scenario, I think the worst that could go wrong would be for her to respond and tell me to essentially know my place wayyyyy down in the hierarchy and to never bother her again. Okay, admittedly that might be unpleasant, awkward and make me feel bad. But it wasn't as if she would have me fired for having sent an email passing along the dean's greetings. So not great, but fine. The more likely scenario was that she'd be too busy to respond and would just ignore me. Also, fine. *Best case* was that I'd get to know the lead lawyer at our firm, and it might lead to something else. I was surprised and delighted that it was the latter scenario that played out. She became an incredible mentor and friend and even ended up officiating at my wedding when she was an appellate judge. Point is that sometimes you have to take a calculated risk and put yourself out there. Often, when you really think through your options and potential outcomes, there really isn't much downside to putting yourself out there and cracking open what could be a door to opportunity.

The power of relationships and friendships became a theme during law school, starting with my small section. Each 1L was assigned to a small group of about 25 students for one of the required classes the first semester of law school. While this may be common today, at the time it was still a relatively novel concept. It gave students an opportunity to get to know other students in a smaller setting that might have seemed more like an upper division class in undergrad. The professors for those small section classes were also specially selected based, one assumes, on their excellent teaching ability and ability to help 1Ls settle into the law school educational environment – it was most assuredly **not** because they were easy. Each small section was then combined with several other small sections for other required 1L courses. As a result, by the end of that first year, we knew most of the other students in our class as well as a few 2Ls and 3Ls.

I really enjoyed this approach, though having been at a large school like NIU and also having been to graduate school, I may have been less intimidated by the academic rigor expected than others. My small selection was Torts and I quickly became friends with four other female students which we (or maybe it was just me) referred to as the Group o' Five Chicks. We have remained friends to this day despite being in vastly different areas of work and scattered a bit across the country. We helped each other when we had personal issues, questions about a class, creation and sharing of the ever-important outlines, and to maintain a sense of humor in the midst of a lot of work.

In law school, the overachieving students who manage to also be really annoying (you know, the ones who sit at the front of the class and are always raising their hands and asking questions to curry favor with the professors) are referred to as gunners. In our property law class, there was such a large number of gunners that it was beyond obnoxious. So, being smart ladies with a bit of sarcasm, we created the concept of property law boyfriends.

No, don't worry, we weren't indicating in any way that these boyfriends would BE our property (because that would be slavery, which is still officially illegal in the United States), only that they would be our boyfriends for property law class. And, Madison and UW being progressive environments, "boyfriends" could be of any gender. Our jobs as girlfriends was to feel our hearts swell with pride at the quantity (not quality, clearly) of stuff that spewed from the mouths of our respective boyfriends, yet not gag. And cast knowing, proud looks at the girlfriends of the other property law boyfriends. "Oh, yes, he's mine, all mine...."[21]

Now, it just so happened that during the semester we were taking property law, I was in the process of buying my first home, a townhouse in the near suburbs of Milwaukee, both for investment purposes and so I would not have to travel back and forth from Madison to Milwaukee every day during the summer while I was working full time. (It also indicates how affordable housing was in Milwaukee that I could do this while only working part-time). There was a clause in the homeowners' association document that I didn't quite understand, so I visited the professor during her office hours to, essentially, request what I now realize amounted to free legal assistance. She was an amazing professor and walked me through the clause and confirmed there was nothing to worry about. She then asked how I was finding the class and in responding about how interesting I found it since it was so practical, I inadvertently mentioned that such interest was despite the performance of my property law boyfriend.

"Your what?"

Uh oh.

Now this particular professor was a true feminist. She had a partnership, but not marriage, with the father of her son. She wrote a book about the politics of sex and articles on

---

[21] *Not to be sexist, but there weren't any annoying female gunners that were at the level of unpleasantness required for consideration as a property law boyfriend/girlfriend.*

the tort of seduction.[22] She also had a good sense of both humor and whimsy and was a bit adventurous, particularly when it came to birding vacations. Her cat, Fred, also featured prominently in her property law examples. In short, she was amazing, but not intimidating. Yet I was intimidated at this particular point in time because of my own stupidity.[23]

So I was just honest with her, explaining the whole game and that we were gearing up for the championship round in which, during the final week of lectures, we would keep track of contributions of our respective property law boyfriends and award the Cool School Ken Barbie doll to the winning girlfriend.

There was a pause. And a small smirk.

And then she just HOWLED. When she stopped laughing, she lowered her voice and said, "Now, I'm not saying I condone this type of game in my classroom because property law is no laughing matter, particularly to the many people who are not afforded the protections of the law. I do appreciate the gender equity component, though. And the creativity. Would you mind letting me know who wins? After finals, of course."

Of course....

---

[22] *When many people hear the word "tort," they often think of "torte" the dessert. It takes a while to get used to spelling tort correctly, particularly when hungry. I have to admit, though, Torte of Seduction sounds like something that would sell very well at a bakery. You know, right next to goods that are "sinfully rich."*

[23] *This is also a good reminder of a concept I learned later (albeit in a business context), the "Wall Street Journal Rule." In a nutshell, if you wouldn't be willing to have something splashed on the front page of that or another reputable publication, you should probably not be engaging in whatever you're thinking of doing as it is bound to come out at some point in time, often when you least expect it.*

I also maintained a running list of the fascinating and glorious shoes our civil procedure professor displayed (with only a few repeats during the semester – what a closet she must have) as well as a list of Cliffisms from our contract law professor. (My favorite was "Don't wrestle with a pig in the mud because you'll get dirty. And pigs like that.")

Being Yourself Resonates

Each of these professors, in their own way, were allowing their authentic selves to shine through. Whether you enjoy or are alarmed by a professor unbuttoning his dress shirt to display a Tango Argentina t-shirt (which related to one of the day's cases) beneath, you have to respect that Cliff was "all in" when he did that. The same was true with the others. The willingness to be vulnerable and authentic has such an amazing way of establishing a level of trust and belief that even if you may not entirely agree with them, you can develop a mutual level of respect.

To be authentic, though, you must first know yourself and who you are, and then have the confidence to open yourself up to others, whether wearing an in-your-face pair of shoes that are obvious or introducing birding adventures into casual conversation. Life Success Factors can help with understanding who you are (though that also involves a good amount of introspection and reflection). And seeing growth based on alignment with your Life Success Factors will help feed your self-confidence to give you the courage to live authentically.

So, we tried to introduce humor where we could, but let's face it – it was a long, grinding slog. Take reading, for example. As you know by now, I've always really enjoyed reading. I knew that there was supposed to be a lot of reading in law school, so yet another reason to love it, right? Or not. I was used to technical reading from graduate school and could easily do 60 pages per night without any issue. Law school was much more intense. Sixty pages would have been a light night of reading **per class**, not overall. And there were multiple classes. And with that awesome Socratic Method, I could be called upon at any time to not just know things at a higher level than I could by skimming the reading, but I needed to be prepared to present the facts of the case and debate it. I had neither time to read anything for pleasure nor any inclination to pick up anything to read if it was not absolutely required. I came to dread reading, one of my true pleasures in life. After law school, it took well over a year before I was interested in picking up a book for fun because the joy of reading had left me during law school. The reading thing also had a spillover effect at work, where I needed to do a fair amount of reading to keep up on what was going on in the world of computer forensics and electronic evidence. It was a real struggle. I was just soooooo tired of reading.

How could my love of learning bring me such grief? Was it really a life success factor if this was how so much reading made me feel? No. And that's where how you specifically define your life success factor is critical. That life success factor for me is "active exploration," meaning I choose what I want to explore. Yes, there is learning involved, but learning by itself is not the objective. It's the ability to seek out things that are interesting to me. And, I can't lie, criminal procedure was not an area I felt compelled to actively explore. But it had to be done.

This is really important. Sometimes we have to just suck it up and get through things because they are part of the path to accomplishing our life vision. It's the goals part of achieving our life vision. You think through those goals, how they will support your life vision and whether they are in alignment with your life success factors. Life isn't easy. Parts are full of hard, dull work, but you do it because you know you are growing and working towards something bigger that is necessary for what you want to accomplish in life. Like getting a law degree. And the struggle makes the achievement of the goal even that more meaningful.

When it comes to the gritty work of creating an amazing life, it's helpful to have a place to which you can retreat and just hunker down. During my law school years, my place was a small table in the basement of the law library. There was no artwork, nothing to detract me other than the lights in the stacks that were motion sensitive (yet seemed to turn on and off without the presence of others unless ghosts were moving among the stacks). Just the slightly musty smell of books, a creaky chair, the far-off rumbling of the elevator, and a strong WiFi connection. Sure, I did my classwork there, but it was also the place where I could be safe just staring into space a bit and thinking, breathing, imagining. I didn't own it, yet it had a weird feeling of home about it. And surprisingly, I think I only ever encountered someone else at that desk once when I wanted to use it.

Towards the end of my first year, the townhouse in Milwaukee became my other retreat on weekends. There, I could feel myself physically separating from the stress and demands of law school. It allowed me to get grounded in my work and in other aspects of my life. It also ended up being a sort of outpost for the Group o' Five Chicks. One summer, two of my classmates were doing internships in Milwaukee, so one stayed in the second bedroom and the other in the finished basement. I was working on a project out of town most of the summer, so I hardly saw them as they would return home to Madison on weekends.[24] The last year of law school, I theoretically shared the apartment with the husband of another Chick. He was a public defender, so he stayed at my place Monday through Thursday nights while he worked in Milwaukee and then went home to Madison on the weekends. It was perfect since I was basically only in Milwaukee on weekends.

Suffice it to say, your space doesn't have to be much, and it doesn't have to be exclusively yours, but I highly encourage you to find it. A place that is yours. Where you can do what needs to be done. And let your mind wander to what you want your life to be and plan how to get there. And, yes, perhaps even re-assess where you are with your life success

---

[24] *The fiancé of one of the chicks was a police officer who had various days off. He would come to Milwaukee some of those days so that he could spend time with the chick in her off hours. He asked once if there was anything he could do to help around the house. One project I said I could really use his help with was disassembling the nasty pressboard entertainment center in the basement left behind by the previous owners. It had been hand-painted (with a paintbrush, not as if it were decorative paint applied by hand) a flat black. Hideous. So, he ripped it apart, lugged the pieces upstairs and pitched them into the dumpster. The elderly single woman next door approached me one evening as I came home, noting that she had seen a young man carrying things out of my house and was I aware of this? I explained the situation and that said young man was actually an off-duty police officer. She apparently was very plugged into the neighborhood gossip, but her hearing aid may not have been as switched on because I soon "learned" that I was going to be marrying a police officer! Also, we needed to re-consider our neighborhood watch program if a police officer were moving in. I loved that neighborhood. I think my home ownership there brought the average age down to at least 55.*

factors and whether it's time to create or modify your goals to help move the needle.

Some of the things I spent a fair amount of time thinking about in the basement of the law library were what classes I should take.

As in undergraduate, there are certain classes that you must take in law school.[25] Things like civil procedure, criminal procedure, constitutional law, legal writing, torts, contracts, property law and the like. Once you're past the largely scripted first year, you have more flexibility in determining what to take, whether you will pursue a specialization, etc. While I tried to branch out a bit, it was clear from the beginning that I was still drawn to all things business. Courses like international trade law, antitrust law and, of course, securities regulation, lit me up. And what should be more natural for a business-loving CPA than tax law?

A lot of things, as it turned out. Remember how in undergrad I loved tax and wanted to get my Master in Tax? And then realized I hated tax and switched to a Master in

---

[25] *The series of required courses was particularly important because of the "diploma privilege" in Wisconsin. Under a Wisconsin Supreme Court rule, those receiving the Juris Doctor degree from an ABA accredited law school in the state -- UW Law and Marquette University -- who take a certain series of courses that would normally be covered in a bar exam, are admitted to the bar so long as they also meet the character and fitness requirements. So, if you're planning to practice law in Wisconsin, it is a great advantage. I ended up taking the bar exam in Illinois since one generally cannot "waive" into another jurisdiction absent a history of practicing law in Wisconsin, and even then, many other states still require taking a bar exam. There is, or at least was, a sort of loophole, in that those serving as federal judicial clerks or working for the federal government often only needed to be admitted to a state to work there and, after working in that capacity, might be able to waive into the state in which the federal job was located.*

Accounting Science with emphasis in Accounting Information Systems? And I'd taken another tax course in the master's program and continued to hate it. But surely now that I was an actual CPA and had matured, it would be easier and I'd take to it like a duck to water, right? No, more like a duck with an anchor chained to her foot. What made it even worse was that my classmates thought I was kind of faking it because, well, duh, of course I should be good at tax.[26]

Except that I wasn't. No matter how hard I tried or how great the professor, I finally accepted that tax was not my thing, had never really been my thing and never would be my thing. Yet despite evidence of all of this, I had doggedly forged ahead, forcing myself into this realm that never really seemed comfortable. Because I bought into the idea of "should." That I *should* be good at one area of law because it related to another area of business that I was quite good at. That I *should* take tax because it was part of the breadth of business offerings – even if I didn't enjoy it and had no intention of ever being a tax attorney. That perhaps I *should* take tax because it was more of a sure thing in a public accounting firm than computer forensics.

---

[26] *One of the things that drives many accountants nuts is that when we say we're accountants, people immediately start asking tax questions. As if that's all we do (if we do it at all). They refer to tax busy season, which isn't the same thing as audit busy season. My quip in response to this before I bought my condo was that I still completed the 1040-EZ form (true) so if their situation was more complicated than a simple W-2, they should probably seek professional assistance. When I bought the townhouse in Milwaukee, I had to file the 1040-A form for the first time because I finally had mortgage interest and local property tax deductions. Now, I'm not capable of much more than providing summary information with supporting documentation to a real tax guy who figures out the rest.*

Few good things come out of a conversation that begins with "you should" unless the "should" is related to your life success factors or a long-term goal you are working towards. The worst part about taking tax in law school was I did it because of what **I** thought the shoulds were, rather than anyone else expressing those shoulds. It was all in my head. Because I didn't have life success factors at that time, I didn't realize that this type of learning wasn't active exploration, that I definitely didn't want to teach tax to someone else, that there was very little creativity involved, that beating my head against the wall was counterproductive to at least mental fitness, and that there was no way I would ever try to derive financial stability from tax, so there was zero reason to take the course.

There's a familiar saying, "If at first you don't succeed, try, try again." I can't say that I agree with that second "try." We don't always succeed when we try something for the first time. In fact, it is the struggle of getting better that leads to mastery, and that takes a lot of practice. So, it's good to try again – IF you are convinced that the topic is related to a longer-term interest of yours or a necessary interim step.

We are more open (and ready) to certain ideas and experiences at certain points in our lives, so it absolutely makes sense that something may not make sense right now but might be a good fit later on. I hated beets as a child but was willing to try them again as an adult and it turns out I love them now. But if I loved my first tax course, hated the second tax course in undergrad to the extent that I changed graduate school plans, tried again anyway in graduate school and still hated it, was there really any doubt what will happen when I tried it a third time in law school? Nope. Yet I listened to my mental chatter about what I *should* do and signed up. And hated it yet again, despite an amazing professor.

There's much to be said for having a stick-to-it approach to life. So long as you are *choosing* what you are sticking to. When you understand your life success factors, you will know when you're pushing yourself, willing something to happen, stubbornly forcing something to happen, because of some sort of "should." If, however, you have an intense amount of curiosity, passion and motivation in a particular area, that's when you drill down and grind it out. Because you're pursuing your passion. Doesn't mean that you won't still have some challenges – you will – but you'll know that you're the one forcing the issue, not the "shoulds" of life. I eventually did realize tax was not my thing, but still kick myself for the decision to enroll in a tax course when I could have doubled down on international trade law or another interesting topic instead.

Despite the waste of time on the tax class, I did manage to fit in quite a few classes that really piqued my interest in various areas of the law. That, in turn, made me wonder whether I should stay with the firm after I graduated or if I should try out the law firm life. I decided to dip a toe into the water and at least participate in some interviews for summer internships. It went about as well as my summer internship interviews when I was in graduate school.

For starters, it seemed somewhat awkward for the interviewers and me that most of them were younger and had less work experience than I did. Law firms and accounting firms share some common features since they are both professional services firms, so I started asking the interviewers questions about their role in business development, leverage and training of other professionals, and their approach to client service. After a few blank stares, it occurred to me that I might know more about those topics than they did. Awkward. The interviews didn't go very far – beyond the weirdness of the discussions, there was the glaring fact that, because I worked 20 hours per week, I didn't have the bandwidth to even try out for moot court or law review, let alone make the cut for them. I also wasn't in the top 10 percent of my class, those coveted spots that nearly guarantee you a spot with a top law firm so long as you can walk, talk and chew gum at the same time.

I would be lying if I said it wasn't ego-bruising to not get very far in the process. I was adult to recognize that I hadn't put in all that other effort that many of my amazing classmates had and, quite frankly, didn't deserve one of those spots because of that. More importantly, I realized I was fine with not advancing since I'd started interviewing in the first place just to test the waters and I already HAD a job. And not just any job, but one that I liked, with amazing colleagues, that paid me well, was challenging and had excellent potential for advancement. So other than putting me behind a year or two behind my colleagues at the firm who had been working full-time versus my part-time schedule while in law school, there wasn't really a downside to having gone to law school. Not to mention, of course, that I was picking up a law degree that most of those colleagues wouldn't have and an extended professional network.

Already having a job always took a tremendous amount of pressure off of me and the experiences I had gained also made me a different law student than I would have been if I had gone to law school straight from undergraduate or graduate school. That background also resulted in me probably being a bit annoying to my classmates because I asked a lot of questions.[27] And not necessarily about things that were in the particular case that we may have been studying. I wanted to know the practicalities when applied to a modern business world, for example. Which fit in well with Wisconsin's Law in Action approach. But when I asked some of these questions, I could easily imagine the other students rolling their eyes. Is it possible that I was *worse* than a gunner? Maybe. But the more I focused on learning and trying to apply what I was learning rather than focusing obsessively on grades, the more I was able to just enjoy the process.

In the midst of that enjoyment, something unexpected arose; our little computer forensics group was moved to be part of another group within the firm called Litigation Advisory Services.

Hmmm. What's that? Sounds like my law school experience, in addition to my computer forensics experience, might fit in well there.

Imagine my surprise when I discovered that this group did forensic accounting investigations. Yes, fraud

---

[27] *To be clear, I do not believe the questions rose to a level that might have qualified me to be eligible as someone's property law girlfriend.*

investigations, the thing I had been pretty much begging to do since I started at the firm. How did I not find this earlier? One reason was that it was a pretty small group and only existed in some of the larger offices. But it was also sometimes difficult to find out much about other service lines within the firm because companies didn't have websites then with that type of information, let alone intranets to provide information within organizations. Crazy now to think of how much information I have at my fingertips, yet sometimes it seems just as difficult to find information I need precisely because there is so *much* information. But I digress.

Because I was doing both computer forensics work as well as data analytics and the latter would stay with the other practice, I was given a choice – I could stay and do data analytics or I could leave data analytics behind and continue to do computer forensics in the new group. From a logical perspective, the choice was relatively easy since I liked doing computer forensics and now, one would assume in a group named Litigation Advisory Services, it seemed like I would also be able to apply my legal knowledge to help our clients who just happened to also be attorneys.[28] It represented active exploration and growth opportunities versus continuing to do the same thing. And if I continued to do the same thing I was doing before I went to law school, then what would have been the point of going to law school in the first place?

At the same time, at a personal level, it wasn't an entirely easy decision because I would be leaving the team that had supported me from the time I pitched the idea of an

---

[28] *Just to be clear, I do not practice law at the firm as part of my client serving activities, which would be prohibited under legal ethics rules.*

internship through my staff years and through law school. I felt like I would somehow be betraying them if I chose the other group. I needn't have worried. The same team spirit and support for my career that they had shown along the way was still there and they encouraged me to take the offer to join the new group. I think they may have realized more than I did at the time that my law degree would not have been as relevant in the existing position and that, well, I had grown as a professional. And it wasn't as if I were leaving the firm and going to a competitor.

I'm not sure that I handled the transition as professionally as I would have liked, but the way that Bill and others encouraged me was certainly a lesson in grace, growth and support. And every time I see one of my former colleagues, it is like seeing family.[29]

The remainder of law school passed by in a continuing blur and graduation arrived before I knew what was happening. While my classmates were heading out to make their mark and, for most of them, hold down their first full-time job, I was returning to the firm full-time, but with exciting new opportunities in a different practice, so it was a new beginning for me as well. I couldn't wait to start.

---

[29] *A few years ago, Bill retired and invited me to his retirement party. I was honored to be included and would not have missed it for the world. It was truly like a family reunion, seeing current and former colleagues whose lives he had impacted and telling stories from back in the day and boring our respective significant others something silly.*

Chapter 6 – Prioritizing and Managing Life Success Factors

"Opportunities abound, but one must still find and open doors."

LAW SCHOOL WAS A SORT OF crucible for me. While I chose to go to law school, the experience and learning changed me and my outlook in ways that I had not anticipated, some positive, others not. I had no concept of life success factors when I started law school, nor when I emerged. Yet when I look back, the steps that led me to law school and some of the features of law school itself did align with some of what I now see as my life success factors. I fell flat on some of them. As I mentioned earlier, I didn't take steps to keep fit during law school. This lack of fitness and the stress that tends to go hand in hand with law school eventually led to nearly debilitating migraine headaches as well as lower back issues, which required a lot of attention to address and manage them during law school so that they didn't become longer-term concerns. I also did virtually nothing for my creativity life success factor (being able to argue both sides of a case in a legal brief is not exactly the type of creative writing that I find enjoyable in my spare time).

Parts of my life atrophied during law school because I didn't take the time to care for and exercise them. Along the way in my very active childhood, I broke an arm and, later, a foot, both of which required heavy plaster casts. I was fascinated when the casts came off at how the broken limb had turned skinny and scrawny while in the cast because they weren't being used like the other one. Same deal with life success factors. You can ignore them for a while, but when you realize that they're missing from your life, it takes a lot more effort to bring them back to your life. But it will be soooo worth it.

A few chapters ago, I asked you to think about what your life success factors might be. Hopefully, you've come up with some ideas. Let's revisit them now, refine them, and give them a reality check.

Definition

When defining your life success factors, precision is important so that you know exactly what you mean by the factor. That does not mean that they should be long or detailed. Instead, they should be very succinct, generally just a few words. Aim for bullet points, not paragraphs. When you see each point, it should be immediately clear to you what the point represents. And it should pretty much make you smile as you read it because it is YOU. The word or phrase might not be crystal clear to a stranger reading them, but they're for you, not that stranger. Also, you should be able to easily rattle off what your life success factors are without having to stop and think about them, which is easier to do with 10-15 words than with 30 or more.

Your life success factors are essentially the elements of the elevator speech of your life. If you haven't encountered that concept before, it is basically a canned description of your project, role, company that you could easily explain to someone in the course of an elevator ride. So, when you look at your bullet list of life success factors, think of how and whether it would be easy for you to quickly translate them to explain to others what is essential for you in life.

I recommend writing your life success factors on a 3 x 5 index card (or a sticky note – whatever you have handy, but preferably not digital as you want something that you keep coming across, rather than something you have to remember to look at). Carry them around with you for a week or two. Take them out and look at them from time to time and see if they still make sense or if you need to modify them. And start thinking of your elevator speech that incorporates the life success factors into your description of what is important for you to achieve a satisfying and fulfilling life.

Life Success Factor Versus Goal

Take a look at each life success factor and make sure none are goals disguised as life success factors. One of the easiest ways to determine this is to ask whether the item can be achieved or acquired. If so, it is a goal. If you have something that is a goal, take a closer look at why you want to achieve that goal and what happens after you reach it. That may help you see the larger idea and life success factor that lies behind the goal.

Purpose

As with goals, life success factors are also not the same as one's purpose, but they will likely be closely related. There has been an explosion of books on purpose recently, both on a personal level as well as for businesses. I have read several of them, and will continue to read them because while it seems like I am supposed *(and you know how I feel about what society says we "should" want or have) to have one single, unifying purpose, I haven't found it yet.*

The concept of purpose generally seems to be combined with a concept of service, of giving back, of being a part of something larger than oneself, of leaving a mark on the world that matters. Even if you've only spent a half day doing a mandatory community service day, you probably realize how good it feels to give back. If you identify a particular area of service on which you want to focus, you would likely be getting this feeling of satisfaction on a regular basis, and it might become your singular focus. But while doing something on a persistent basis because it brings you happiness and fulfillment meets the concept of a life success factor, having a purpose is more than that. The best that I can describe it (again, nothing having a single, driving purpose myself), is that purpose may represent an alignment of your life success factors in one overriding direction or activity.

*But let me also offer a caution here. If **all** of your life success factors are truly aligned in your purpose, that's fantastic. But if you allow your purpose to pull you along rather than being guided by **all** of your life success factors, it can be just as easy to become misaligned with your life success factors when you have a purpose as when you do not have a purpose. We have all seen amazing figures who have worked in science, education, philanthropy and other areas where they have a laser focus on their purpose, but are so wrapped up in that work that they have not taken care of their health or maintained healthy relationships with family and friends, and may wind up unhappy. Balance and maintaining alignment are key to lasting happiness and fulfillment.*

Ask a Friend

Once you have a refined list of your life success factors, try bouncing it off of a trusted family member or a friend who has known you for at least a few years. Give them your elevator speech and then go into further detail as relevant. Friends and family often see patterns that we may be too close to ourselves to really see. Explain that you're crafting life success factors to help guide you toward a life that satisfies and fulfills you. If you found photos during your brainstorming exercise, you might want to share those as well.

For each factor, ask if they can think of examples from your life when you were really happy and fulfilled and that factor was at play. Some individuals may only be able to comment on a few factors if they only see part of your life. For example, work colleagues or classmates where you have limited interaction may not know much about what you do in your personal life, whereas your parents or siblings may not have good visibility of what excites you in your academic or professional life. If they provide examples in addition to the ones that you've thought of for a particular factor, that's a good indicator that the area is indeed important to you and perhaps also that you are successful at nurturing it.

If they aren't able to come up with additional examples, that doesn't mean that it isn't a life success factor for you. It may only mean that you haven't spent as much time nurturing it and it may need to be a greater area of focus moving forward. But if multiple people who know you well not only cannot think of examples on a point but think that the factor doesn't sound like the kind of person they know as you, you may want to think about the factor a bit more. Is it an area where you have always wanted to be or do something but haven't found the freedom, resources or courage to act on it? Is it an area where someone may have told you that you're not good at a particular thing or some other type of negative thought that prevented you from pursuing that factor? Is it an area where you think it *should* be one of your factors? Remember that the factors relate to the type of life you **want** to pursue, so dig deep and listen to yourself.

One other thing you'll want to ask your trusted friend is whether she can think of other factors that should be on your list. Friends and family members have often seen the best and worst of us and may have a better perspective for helping tease out the things that light us up.

Gaps and Moving Forward

Now that you have begun fine-tuning your life success factors, take inventory of where you are with those factors. When you began identifying your factors, you thought back to things that made you happy and fulfilled in the past. Now add in the examples and input from friends and family. Move your focus towards the present. Are you frequently touching on each life factor? Are some in need of more concerted effort and attention to get you back on track to achieving happiness and fulfillment in that aspect of your life?

The simple diagnostic below can serve as a tool to help you assess where you are with each of your factors and where you want to go. This will form the basis for future chapters where you will begin to outline your life vision and set goals to move you there.

1. Identify Relative Importance

First, identify the relative importance of each of your life success factors where 1 is the least important. For example, if you have four life success factors, the most important will receive a score of four, whereas the least important will have a score of one. Your most important life success factor would be something you might describe as important to have present in your life on a near-daily basis or essential to your being. Your least important, while still important enough to merit being a life success factor, might, on the other hand, be described as something that always brings me pleasure and I need to experience on a periodic basis.

In my world, active exploration is the most important of my life success factors. If I don't learn something each day, I consider the day a disappointment. Creativity, on the other hand, may be something that I need just a few times per month. Or put another way, what are your must-haves versus nice-to-haves?

2. Assess Satisfaction

Next, we want to look at how you feel you have been doing with each of your life success factors in the past as well as currently. When looking at your past success, ask yourself the extent to which the factor has been present in your life. Then, for your current status, consider how happy you are with how present the factor is in your life now. Assess each life success factor accordingly based on the following scale:

1: Not at all

2: Not very often

3: Sometimes

4: Frequently

5: Almost all of the time

3. Calculate the Gap

Now, calculate the gap for each life success factor. The gap is the difference between your past success and current status. A positive number indicates that you have lost some traction on the factor, whereas a negative factor indicates that you have been actively improving. The gap and its direction only reflects success in aligning your life with the life success factor; it does not suggest something really is a life success factor or not.

4. Determine Priority

Finally, multiply the gap score by the importance score to determine relative priority for each of the factors for future goal planning.

Table 2

Life success factor	Relative importance	Past success (1-5)	Current status (1-5)	Gap (Past – Current)	Priority (Importance x Gap)

You are not bound by the priority score, but it helps magnify the gaps to indicate some good places to focus your energy and intention going forward.

Continue to review and refine your life success factors. You may want to consider the chart above on a daily or weekly basis as well at the outset to get a sense of when you have good days whether they are also hitting on multiple life success factors. The more experience you have comparing your life success factors to how you feel about your growth, the more you can narrow and focus those factors.

Chapter 7 – Applying Life Success Factors to Create Goals

*"Visualizing your future has a higher rate of
return than reflecting on your past."*

I ENJOYED MY TIME IN LAW SCHOOL, but it was so nice once I was out to not have to divide my time and attention between law school and work and the priorities and deadlines that always seemed to collide. That's not to say that life beyond law school was a cake walk. Just the contrary. I was energized being in the new practice, but I also had a lot to learn. I threw myself into meeting others within the practice and expanding my professional network as well as learning about the additional services that the new group provided beyond computer forensics. I was a weird combination of being like a kid in a candy shop and drinking from a fire hose those first few months.

On the personal side, I also saw that it would be necessary to sell my place in Milwaukee (yes, my happy place) and move back to the Chicago area because there was no one else from the practice in Milwaukee (and this was before much work was done virtually). Real estate prices are much higher in Chicago than in Milwaukee, so I had to take a step backward from home ownership and rent for a couple years until I had saved up enough money for a down payment on a condo. That turned out to be a great decision as I ended up traveling a good share of the time and wouldn't have had much time for home ownership responsibilities.

After a while, though, I became familiar with the flow of things and started to get a bit restless. My energy was no longer directed and was leaking out rather than propelling me along. It was time to think about where I wanted to go and, well, develop some goals.

When I was an undergraduate, I invested in a Hewlett Packard Business Consultant II device. Some might look at it now and call it a glorified calculator, but for the early '90s, it was much more than a calculator. It's hard to describe it (but do a search online for HP 19BII and you'll get the idea), but it had a multiple-line display, the ability to do histograms and some graphs and – here's the key – store lists. I had read that you were more likely to achieve your goals if you wrote them down, and the more specific the more likely to be achieved, so I decided to input my goals into a stored list. Genius, right? Yeah, not so much. Because when the non-rechargeable battery had to be replaced, all my data was lost. Doh!

I do remember a few of the goals, though.

- Make $60,000 a year by the time I was 30
- Own a two-story house with garage, yard and trees by the time I was 35
- Work in international business, including living abroad and learning another language
- Write a book

Now these are clearly all goals and not life success factors. But I look back at them now and smile because they indicate a direction in life that I wanted to go. I wanted to explore, be financially successful, but also give something back. In other words, they sound an awful lot like my life success factors. Which makes sense because the life success factors are supposed to guide us to our life visions through incremental goals.

After law school, as I started to think about where I wanted my life to go, I revisited those goals and thought about what else I might want to accomplish. A year or so after graduation, I had been promoted to senior manager, which is the next step before partner. Based on my experience up to that point (and I'd say the same thing now), making partner is not easy; it's hard work on a variety of levels. Did I really want to stick around for that? It also was clear to me that if I wanted to actually practice law, I would need to leave the firm and do so sooner rather than later while my legal knowledge and training were still relatively fresh. Hmmm....

This is the point at which I was able to score the time on my mentor's calendar and developed the life success factors in preparation for that meeting. In addition to her leadership position at the firm, I was particularly interested in her perspective because she had left the firm to take a position in government and had returned to the firm after that. While she wasn't a lawyer, her experience working in government surrounded by lawyers and deciding to return were about as on point as I could think.

She appeared to genuinely like the approach of the life success factors (though as noted earlier, she did ask where family and friends were on the list, which is why it's a good idea to stress test your factors with friends and family who know you). And she provided excellent counsel. She noted that some life success factors are easier to touch on a regular basis so it's easier to feel success and satisfaction. Others may be more nuanced, and you might not get a direct hit frequently, so they may require a bit more motivation and staying power. Knowing the difference matters, which is why prioritizing your life success factors in terms of which you need on a more frequent basis is important.

This reminds me a bit of Maslow's Hierarchy of Needs. As a refresher, at the base of his pyramid are physiological needs (e.g. food, water, shelter). As you move up, you have safety, belonging/love, self-esteem and, at the top, self-actualization. At this point in time, it's relatively easy in developed countries to obtain the needs at the base level, but things up towards the top may seem out-of-reach for all but those blessed with a lot of free time and resources. So, if you have a life success factor of being able to provide a comfortable lifestyle for your family, that may be somewhat easier to achieve than, say, having a leading online personal brand that would be up in the self-esteem section. Neither factor is better than the other, but the frequency of achieving satisfaction in them may differ.

This may also play into how many life success factors you have. If you only have three life success factors, and two of them are going to be less frequently touched in your life, it could be a bit demoralizing on a day-to-day basis to not get that "hit." But if you have a mixture of factors, some of which are a bit easier, for lack of a better term, and others that are more challenging, it would seem easier to keep on track, and moving forward with all of them, as the easier ones would tide you over during times when you may be having difficulty in other areas. As in investing, diversification is a good thing.

As may be obvious by now, after speaking with the mentor and others, I decided to stay with the firm. The next step was to really dial in on my life success factors and try to align them with my life vision and then work towards getting to that vision through setting intermediate goals. Well, at least that's what I see now. But I didn't really have a life vision at the time, but at least I had a target – making partner.

As a new senior manager, it was likely that I still had at least five years before I might be considered for partner. A typical partnership business case includes a history of delivering excellent service, maintaining quality standards, possessing significant expertise in at least one area, satisfied clients, efficient projects, counseling and mentoring other professionals, developing thought leadership and, of course, having a book of business or revenue stream. Not requiring sleep and being able to juggle and tap dance while singing karaoke are also helpful.

Seeing this tall mountain ahead of me, I tried to break it down into bite-sized pieces while also considering how I could touch on all of my life success factors.

Creativity

When I initially envisioned investigating fraud, I thought of it as part of the financial audits and a relatively straightforward set of procedures that one would perform to determine whether, in fact, fraud had occurred. The reality could hardly have been more different. The projects in the forensics practice were much different and more dynamic. While it's true that projects could arise from a financial audit, they were more likely to emerge from tips from whistleblower hotlines, employees noting that something seemed odd, analytic reviews that identified anomalies and, of course, government or regulatory investigations such as the Securities and Exchange Commission (SEC), Department of Justice (DOJ) or various inspectors general.

Each one had a different starting point and limited set of facts, allegations, opinions, rumors, company politics and personalities operating under a cloak of secrecy, confidentiality and mystery. Sounds like fun – and it was – but it was also very tricky because you didn't know whether you really had facts, opinions or downright lies. The objectives could vary widely as well. For purposes of attorney-client privilege and attorney work product protection (at least in the United States), we generally worked for either outside lawyers or in-house counsel. It was counsel's job to advise the company; we worked with counsel to gather facts, particularly as they related to financial transactions recorded in the accounting books and records. We did not issue any opinions about the guilt or innocence of companies or individuals but presented the facts we had identified. The lawyers used that information along with other information they gathered to help the client.

Let's take a hypothetical example where a company's internal audit team performs an audit of a US location. During the audit, they run across a series of unusual transactions with a vendor located in Cyprus that appears related to a large project the company is bidding on in

Ukraine. Internal Audit gathers as much information as they can about the transactions but are unable to obtain satisfactory responses from management and some individuals who have left, and some of the documents are in Greek. They report this finding to the company's audit committee, which is concerned since the project pursuit is so significant. The audit committee engages outside counsel to investigate.

Outside counsel would hire us to assist in figuring out what the company paid for, what was received, and how this was reflected in the accounting records. We might do procedures like reviewing the information that internal audit had gathered, participate with outside counsel in interviews of individuals who may have additional information, analyze the accounts to which the transactions were booked in the accounting records, review electronic evidence from the hard drives of individuals or email records, and have our colleagues in Greece or Cyprus perform some procedures related to the Cypriot entity, the ownership or executives of the entity, or the documents that are in Greek.

We might then look at the facts that arose out of these procedures:

- A contract for services by the Cypriot entity, but with no evidence of any services having been delivered
- Payments made to the vendor classified as freight charges, but with no reference to a sales order
- Freight charges to this vendor were at least $25,000 and were always round amounts, compared to average freight charges of $3,294.31

These factors would then cause us to ask more questions and potentially perform more procedures:

- Are there any other vendors with even amounts? Who are they and what do we know about them?
- If the average freight charges were $3,294.31, how many freight charges were significantly higher than that? Were they all one-offs or with a handful of other entities? What do we know about those entities?
- How many freight charges did not reference a sales order? Is there any reason why a sales order would not be referenced for freight charges as part of the standard shipping process?
- Does the vendor have a website? Does it indicate a location? If we look at online maps, does it appear to be a bona fide address for a shipping company or its corporate offices or is it possibly a residence or a rental mailbox location?

Additional research on the Cypriot entity might indicate that it appears to be only one individual versus a real company, that individual is the wife of a Ukrainian government official and that official happens to be on the committee that reviews and grants contracts. Review of e-mails might show that two individuals at the company have exchanged emails referring to particular projects that no one else in the company has heard of. One of those individuals is in sales and the other is an accounting clerk.

Someone looking at the facts might deduce that the two individuals were passing bribes to a government official through this third party (the government official's wife) in order to influence the official to award the project to the company. But that would be a conclusion that we would not draw as we would only summarize the facts gathered, as well as potential additional steps to take. For example, what about payments to other vendors for freight charges? Should more emails be reviewed to see if anyone else had mentioned the project name that the sales representative and accounting clerk had noted? Could this same pattern have been used for other projects? And this only came out of one internal audit for one subsidiary, so could there be similar challenges at other subsidiaries?

Creativity was part and parcel of every project, kind of like the LSAT logic problems in a corporate setting. What might have happened? What might people have done to try to cover up or obscure transactions or events? How did we know who had been involved? What evidence was available? How could we obtain more information on the financial records and transactions? Was there a pattern developing? Could we extrapolate what we learned from one potential transaction to identify a potential scope of fraud, misstatement or corruption?

No two projects were alike, though certainly the skills learned on one project could be applied to others. Another area was determining how to apply data analytics to help us solve problems and dashboards incorporating artificial intelligence to help clients identify potential trouble spots before they became full-blown problems. So, while I may not have been doing creative activities like performing music, writing, painting or something like that, I was hitting on my creativity life success factor every single day I walked into the office.

Active Exploration

My work performing investigations also really lit up my active exploration life success factor, both because I was learning so much with each engagement, and because they often entailed a significant amount of international travel.

I've been interested in language and international travel for a long time. For some reason, though I wasn't all that intrigued by the issues of *National Geographic Magazine* at home while I was growing up, I found it exotic when I heard of people whose specialization was Russian literature and the like. In fact, I had actually signed up to learn Russian in what would have been my sophomore year at NIU. I should note that this was before the Berlin Wall fell and the Soviet Union began to crumble. But since I transferred to La Sierra University my sophomore year and they didn't offer Russian, I took up French. I had big plans of doing a semester or year abroad in France and then realized if I did so that I would likely lose my music scholarship, making my return a bit expensive. So, I chickened out. And, of course, always regretted it. But I did at least get my passport.

The firm had different programs where you could do a couple years abroad, but with my enrollment in law school around the same time one would normally apply for one of those gigs, the timing just didn't work out for me, so my passport remained disturbingly empty of any stamps. That quickly changed when I started doing investigations. I think it was only my third investigation where it was suddenly necessary for a bunch of people to simultaneously fan out across Europe for a large project. My destination was Sweden. I was stoked. Have passport, will travel. I rushed to the local bookstore and bought some books and media to learn a bit of Swedish and another about business etiquette in other countries because I had no clue. But I wanted to decrease the odds of others catching on to the fact that I'd never been "off the rock" before.

The whole team gathered in London first, so my first border crossing (okay, I'd been to Canada, but that didn't really count because at the time Americans didn't need a passport to cross that border) was relatively painless and was at least in my own language. I experienced my first jetlag, but it was more of a case of being too excited by finally being in another country that I wasn't able to sleep and stayed up wandering around a bit and getting up early to do more of the same. Then the team I was leading (!!) headed to Stockholm. In the dead of winter. With only a few hours of sunlight each day. (We literally drove to work in the dark and came home in the dark so going outside for lunch was our only chance to catch a bit of sunshine.)

I quickly discovered that rental cars in Europe were all manual transmissions, not automatic, and that none of my team members knew how to drive a manual transmission. As a result, I would be putting all those farm girl years of manual transmissions and clutching to work and doing all the driving. I admit that I did so happily because our Saab station wagon (necessary for the four of us and all of our stuff) had studded snow tires. Super fun!

From that point on, I could not get enough of international travel. It didn't matter where, when, with whom or for how long – I and my passport were ready to roll. I became nearly addicted to being places where I had to struggle to figure out what was going on, where I had the opportunity to learn a bit of the language and connect with people I encountered. And, yes, make a fool out of myself from time to time with my mistakes and misunderstandings, but those were almost always met with good humor and forgiveness by the respective country's residents because at least I tried.

While the general knowledge obtained for investigations as well as for different countries was intriguing, it would not on its own be enough of the right kind of learning for me to create a business case to be promoted to partner. For that, I also needed some more in-depth industry and/or technical experience.

Not long after I joined the new practice, we had a semi-annual meeting of all managers, senior managers and partners in the practice, which at the time was probably fewer than 75 people. It happened to start on Super Bowl Sunday and the hotel had set up this somewhat bizarre room with a bunch of inflatable chairs for viewing -- the types of chairs you might have around a pool or for kids. While gazing at this specter, I met a very youthful-looking senior manager, Ted. He had also just joined the group and was creating a team focused on life sciences (whatever that was). I tucked that in the back of my mind because I, obviously, was not focused on that area, but he seemed to have a lot of energy and plans for his team.

Over time as I became more involved in leading investigation teams, Ted asked if I might be interested in joining his team. I explained that I appreciated the invitation, but my knowledge of life sciences was limited to my seasonal use of antihistamines for my allergies. He patiently explained that knowledge wasn't a pre-requisite for joining and that the team, then composed primarily of non-accountants, could really use individuals with accounting expertise and that my legal knowledge would be well-suited for understanding the regulatory environment in which life sciences companies operate.

Hmmm.... Tell me more....

His request actually ended up being somewhat prescient, because shortly after I joined his team, the DOJ and SEC began targeting life sciences companies for potential violations of the Foreign Corrupt Practices Act (FCPA). The FCPA was established in the 1970s following Watergate, and basically prohibits American companies and individuals from making payments or offers to foreign government officials to influence their actions. The example I outlined above might be a typical type of FCPA investigation and it's a relatively straight line from a payment through a third party to the government official who's responsible for approving government contracts. Usually.

The line was not so straight in the case of life sciences. The government's contention was that countries with nationalized health insurance employ doctors and other health care providers. They make decisions on which products to use or prescribe that will be paid or reimbursed by the national government, so they should be considered foreign government officials. So each time a pharmaceutical or medical device sales representative visits a physician's office in, say, France, and offers the physician something (e.g. dinner, food for the front office, prescription drug samples, a trip to a medical conference, a contract to do some research), that could conceivably be considered a bribe to influence him or her to use or prescribe that rep's company's products.

There are a lot of American pharmaceutical and medical device manufacturers with products sold around the world, so this resulted in numerous investigations and I had a front row seat to some of them. This allowed me to develop expertise in this industry sector that, along with my increasing knowledge of investigations, would be helpful in my partnership promotion prospects.

This is also an example of where I was hitting on my life success factor both through my work and in my personal capacity through the travel and language exploration. Of course, as I have noted previously, the more you have all your eggs in one basket for a particular life success factor, the more challenging it may be when that basket is upended. For example, if all of my exploration was tied to my job and I lost my job, I might be a bit adrift for that life success factor. By having developed an intense interest in language and travel that I could pursue independent of work, I had a bit of diversification.

Teaching

The obvious opportunity for teaching is to teach formal classes. While I have yet to teach a course at a university (though I have delivered several lectures through the years),

I did a fair amount of classroom training through our firm's internal training programs. I really enjoyed it and, if the students were being honest in the feedback and ratings they provided, I was pretty good at it.

As I continued to move up through the ranks, I also had the responsibility and opportunity to supervise and mentor other professionals and that's where I was able to really touch on the teaching life success factor nearly daily. There were the day-to-day instructions and discussion about work matters, of course, but being able to develop a level of trust and a sort of mentoring environment often required more than that. When we were out of town (and typically out of the country) on projects, we spent most of our waking hours together. Since the projects were confidential, we couldn't discuss them in public, so we got to really know each other over dinner each night or through tourism on those rare weekends we had time off. Let's just say that you learn a lot about people when you're working late at a client location and get locked in by automatic security gates and none of you speak the local language. (Yes, that actually happened on that first project in Sweden.).

Having shared experiences helped us get through unusual experiences together and with a fair degree of good humor and created friends and colleagues for life. I realized that my team was really important to me. While it is certainly true that the job of a leader is to hire people who are more talented than she is so that everyone can move up to take on more important challenges, I really enjoyed (and continue to enjoy) helping my peeps (my mentees and others with whom I was close) grow. Counseling them on difficult choices on projects or their careers. Seeing them be promoted and taking the next generation under their wings. Taking calls in the middle of the night when they're crying in a hotel room in another country with a client or colleague who's being a jerk. And the joy of someone calling and practically piercing my eardrum when she screamed that she'd passed the CPA exam. Priceless moments I will always remember fondly.

Financial Stability

As I continued to progress in the firm, my compensation increased accordingly. I was able to finally buy a condo in Chicago close to the office and public transit to both airports and start socking away more for retirement. I even bought a small life insurance policy from my brother who was starting an agency, to help him out of course, but to also ensure that, well, if I died suddenly or in some random foreign country, the costs of burial and everything would be taken care of. [Gulp]

With the help of a lawyer (not all lawyers do all types of law, just as not all accountants – ah-hem – are good at taxes), I created a living revocable trust and an estate plan to help provide for the college education of my nieces. And oddly enough, the more that I was traveling, the less that I actually spent because I was rarely home. Which, of course, turned out to be another issue, but was fine from a financial stability perspective.

Health

One of the first things I did after buying my condo was to join the East Bank Club, which is kind of like a resort without hotel rooms. It was just a few blocks from my condo, had multiple pools (including a roof deck pool that was amazing during the summer), two indoor running racks, racquet sports, all the cardio and strength equipment you could imagine, tons of classes, two restaurants, and a spa within the women's locker room. It was, in short, my happy place. On weekends when I was home, I would head there for a morning workout, then have a manicure and sometimes a pedicure or deep tissue massage, and then (after all nails were dried) have a leisurely breakfast/lunch at the grill and then slither my sated, still-greasy, relaxed body back home. It was heaven.

I wasn't crazy fit, but I had a level of fitness that worked for me and kept my weight under control. What it did not – and, in fact, could not – address fully, though was the high level of stress I was under. For the first time in my life, I had some difficulty sleeping. I was always tense (though the massages did help a bit, or so I convinced myself). I started to be short with my colleagues. I couldn't seem to find the time to head out into the suburbs to spend time with my family. The migraines that I had experienced in law school returned. It was not pretty.

A good friend who lived in my building, Renee, was originally from Texas and also happened to be a neuroradiologist. We always joked that she chose neuroradiology since she had no patience for actual humans and didn't have that soothing bedside manner. We were at dinner once while I was in this stress-related funk and she just stopped in the middle of eating her *osso buco* and said (in a thick Texas accent), "Listen, missy, I don't know what you think you're doing, but you're not taking good care of yourself and something is **wrong** with you. If you don't make an appointment and go see your doctor, I'm going to hog-tie you and give you an examination myself." Terrifying in so many ways. So, I went to my doctor who diagnosed me as having a mild depression related to a high level of stress. She said she could prescribe a light dosage of an anti-depressant that might help but thought that seeing a therapist would likely yield better results by just talking through things.

I was *not at all* enthused about the idea of therapy, particularly with all the stigmas that still persisted related to mental health. But it sounded preferable to being hog-tied and examined by Renee, so I tried it out. Two interesting things came out of the therapy sessions. First, I realized how important my peeps were to me, or at least I thought I knew that. But what Stacy, the therapist, noted was that nearly everything I was talking about when describing my levels of stress as well as the things that made me happy related to my peeps. I talked about how I didn't want to let them down, I wanted to work harder to provide a good example to them of what was possible, that I wanted to create opportunities for them, etc. And also, that I felt really guilty about not making time to see my family, which made me think back to my mentor's comment about where friends and family were on my list of life success factors. Hmmm....

So, I updated my life success factors. I combined learning with active exploration to become "active exploration and sharing" because learning without sharing isn't very satisfying. And I added "meaningful relationships" to the list. My point here is that it took an objective third party to help me see what was right in front of my nose. And it is 100 percent fine to update your life success factors as you gain new knowledge.

Soundtrack to Your Life

Another thing that was helpful in therapy (yes, I admit it was helpful) was a piece of homework that I created for myself. In the initial sessions, Stacy was trying to get an understanding of my life and challenges. Well, it would take a long time to go through my 30+ years of life at that point and, being someone who is short on both patience and time and hates to waste money, I decided to cut to the chase.

One night when I was unable to sleep (that hadn't changed), I created the concept of my life's soundtrack. No, not a soundtrack *for* life like white noise or soothing sounds of rainforests or whatever (which, admittedly, I do enjoy, though they didn't help with the sleeplessness), but a soundtrack that would accompany my life if my life were a movie.

In the movie of your life, the scenes will represent the high points, low points and struggles in between that define your life. This links with your life success factors because the high points generally represent the times when your life success factors are in balance. The low points, in contrast, are times when your life is not aligned with your life success factors. In addition, the exercise may be a bit fun and yield a great playlist. Here's how to do it:

- Create an outline of your life like scenes from a movie – a high point, a low point, a moment of challenge or choice.
- Consider whether those scenes represent alignment or divergence from your life success factors or perhaps the existence of another or different life success factor.
- For each of those scenes, choose a piece of music (doesn't matter which genre or even whether it has words) that reminds you of that period of time in your life.
- For extra credit, write "liner notes" as if it were the paper in the old school CD -- a brief sentence or two on each scene.
- Listen to the soundtrack and think of all the amazing things you have done and overcome and revel in how amazing you are.

I recommend ending on a high note like any good movie so that it primes the listener/viewer (you) for the sequel.

Here's an example of the soundtrack from undergrad through my early days at the firm (no laughing at my choice of music, okay?):

- *Elgar: Variations on an Original Theme, Op. 36 "Enigma" – Variation IX (Adagio) "Nimrod"*
  A piece that we played in wind symphony during my freshman year of college at NIU. Powerful piece of music from the beginning of a lot of change in my life.

- *Pie Jesu*, Charlotte Church

  At La Sierra, the wind ensemble toured with a vocal group, the cleverly named Octet. This is one of the pieces they sang. Gives me goose bumps and reminds me of all the great trips we had and friends I made in undergrad.

- *Leaving Port*, "Titanic" Soundtrack

  Listen to the momentum building in this piece and you'll see why I thought it aligned with the momentum of leaving the calm port of academia and heading out into the real world to work.

- *What You Never Know (Won't Hurt You)*, Hayley Westenra

  This one is about the discovery that my boyfriend of four years had cheated on me. That kind of betrayal was hard to take. But I moved on and learned from the experience.

- *What Would Brian Boitano Do?* "South Park: Bigger, Longer & Uncut"

  In the first season of *South Park*, I worked on a project for a few months with all-male colleagues who introduced me to the show and helped me decipher what Cartman was actually saying. I'm not a huge fan, but this song cracks me up and was selected to reflect the process of choosing whether to go to law school.

You get the idea. This isn't something you ever have to share with anyone, but I can almost guarantee that you'll smile every time you listen to your soundtrack and it will be a good reminder of your life success factors in action.

The point of all of this is that, when you take a step back and look at your life, it's full of ups and downs just like any good movie. But the fact that you're thinking about it means you were strong enough to survive them and have a story to tell. It's really important to learn from those ups and downs and, if necessary, reset your virtual compass back to your life success.

Much as I hated the idea of going to therapy and found the experience itself very uncomfortable, it was valuable in helping me through a difficult point in my life and I'm not ashamed to admit that. We all need a bit of help sometimes. I came out of it stronger, pulled myself together, powered through the last months of the partnership process, and then began an agonizing wait to hear whether I had made the cut.

Chapter 8 – Developing and Pursuing a Life Vision

"Focus on your view of life, not the raindrops
that try to block that view."

THE PARTNERSHIP ANNOUNCEMENTS were always made in the week leading up to the U.S. Memorial Holiday Weekend, the last weekend in May. I was told to expect a call. The agonizing part was that it was still entirely possible that I or other candidates wouldn't make it in the final cut based on the strength of the firm and the business units and how many slots our practice might have for new partners. It was a period of high anxiety.

The whole promotion process was shrouded in secrecy so you didn't even tell others on your team that you might be up for partner, both because it was confidential and, well, would you want it to be public that you didn't make the cut if that happened? So that week before Memorial Day, I changed the ringtone on my phone to the BeeGee's song, "Stayin' Alive." (Why, yes, that song is indeed included in my life soundtrack.) Each time my phone rang, I was reminded that I was still alive, as were my partnership prospects, and that it was possible that this could be THE call.

I got the call on a Tuesday and my practice's managing partner confirmed I had made it (Woohoo!!!!!), but the announcement wouldn't go out until that Friday morning so I had to keep it under my hat (at least at the office) for a few more days.

I was scheduled to present at a conference in Paris the week after Memorial Day. When making my travel plans, I realized that, depending on the news, this could either be really good timing or really horrible timing. I decided to head to Paris the same day that the announcement would be made, and also bought a ticket for my Mom to go as well for a few days of tourist activities over the holiday weekend. (And who better to console me than my Mom if things didn't go well or to celebrate if it was good news?)

As we boarded the flight that morning, my phone and e-mail were lighting up with notes of congratulations, which was a great way to start the trip. After the months of stress and hard work, I finally had some downtime, so I was more than happy to accept a pre-take-off thimble of champagne from the flight attendant. Mom, who doesn't drink, invoked my middle name when I did this to apparently publicly shame me for drinking alcohol and doing so in daylight hours (it was early evening). [SIGH] She did, however, let pretty much everyone else in business class and the cabin crew know that her daughter had made partner and that I was taking her to Paris. Simultaneously sweet and horrifying for an introvert who just likes to sink into a quiet cocoon on flights and go unnoticed.

We've talked quite a bit to this point about life success factors and how they figure into our life stories so far, which creates a solid foundation for turning towards how we approach the future. And dreaming and planning for the future requires a life vision. And I do mean "vision" because it needs to be something that you can visualize with a fair degree of clarity with yourself in that picture, front and center.

When you're driving down the road, you have a certain horizon in the distance. The closer you get, the more in focus the specks in the distance become, and a new horizon arises in the distance. It's the same with your life vision. Your life vision should naturally change as you proceed through life based on your achievements and advancements, as well as shifts in the proverbial road that you travel. For example, when you enter a long-term committed relationship or have a child, that may impact not only what your priorities are and what your life will look like, but also requires fitting that other person into your vision. So you have a life vision for what's coming up in the relative short term, a vision for what your future looks like in the longer medium-term, and a vision for how you want today itself to turn out to move you closer to those visions.

My life vision before I made partner was rather myopic as it didn't extend much beyond actually making partner. I'd get promoted, I'd perhaps take a vacation[30] to celebrate and then…. Ummm….?

---

[30] My gift to myself was a seven-day cruise – alone -- to the Mexican Riviera in a cabin with a balcony where I could just read, think, do nothing and watch the waves go by. I somehow thought that by going on a cruise and being at sea, I could be essentially unplugged and out of touch. Imagine my horror when I surfaced early one morning to take pictures of a beautiful sunrise with my BlackBerry's camera (this was pre-smart phone days) only to see the red light blinking that I had mail because we were close enough to the shore for a signal. [SIGH]

Or put another way, I didn't *have* a vision – I had a goal. I had achieved a goal but hadn't given thought to how that fit into a larger picture of my future or my objectives and I didn't really even have goals beyond that one from a career perspective. Part of that was perhaps lack of information to know what actually *being* a partner would entail. But I think it was also that I felt almost paralyzed with the effort required to accomplish what felt like a really big goal that I was just unable or unwilling to try and look beyond that. I didn't have the energy or mental bandwidth to deal with that. The idea of visualizing my life as a partner in a work setting probably would have seemed like a wasteful, indulgent use of my limited time – that's if I had even thought of doing some visualization. And then extending that fanciful daydreaming to my (nearly non-existent at the time) personal life outside of work and then my life even three years behind that? Forget it.

When you allow yourself to be trapped in a sort of prolonged period of flight-or-fight response pattern as I was doing at the time, your body and mind are trained to think only about what is absolutely necessary. Anything else is just nice-to-have and not a priority unless you force yourself to take a step back and think about a life vision. It's easy for me to say this in hindsight, of course. I can see how ridiculous it is that I somehow found time to watch some mindless movie on Netflix but would have considered five minutes to daydream a waste of time. But I didn't have the knowledge and tools at the time to re-align myself. It's clear that I wanted to somehow escape from the discomfort of the reality I was in but didn't realize that I could more productively do that by focusing on a future vision that gave me something positive towards which I could work. Something that may have propelled me forward rather than essentially sheltering in place.

I have come a long way since then, primarily because I have created more focus on my life success factors and leveraged that to create a life vision and the goals to get there. Equally important is establishing a periodic review process to check where I am and re-align if necessary, to get back to a happy place.

On that trip to Paris, I *finally* took a bit of time to think about where I wanted to go next. Being in Paris and soaking up the ambiance of the street cafes, baguettes, art and history, I realized that I really wanted to continue exploring other countries. I also wanted to do more to develop team members, as we often say that the most important job of a partner is to create more partners. Being a partner would give me a platform to help people in different ways as well as to reach more people because I would have multiple teams rather than being focused only on one project at a time. I had this somewhat odd vision of flying around, visiting groups of peeps in different parts of the world, having some great vacations in between, and all while helping clients address their problems. And, in a roundabout way, that's pretty much exactly what happened.

Around this same time, my sister-in-law noted that perhaps I would want to spend more time at home in my condo in Chicago if it felt more like home.

Um, what's wrong with my place?

The condo is a loft with 16-foot high ceilings and no doorways except for bathrooms and closets and at the time was painted white throughout. It felt clean and crisp to me and I had a couple colorful Kandinsky prints hung up that I thought added just the right splash of color. Her response? "Yeah, it's cozy if you like living in a sterile museum."

Ouch.

Now, I would never pretend that I know anything about interior design. And she was right that I never really spent much time there and was always on the go. I pretty much stopped in to do my laundry, see how my cats[31] were, get a healthy meal and a manicure at the East Bank Club, and then I would head out again.

My sister-in-law had a friend who was just starting an interior decorating business and had a knack for understanding people and their priorities, translating that into interiors and doing so at reasonable costs. I figured it couldn't hurt to try. So, we met, and I let her roam around the apartment and storage room where I had some artwork from my travels. When she presented some ideas a few weeks later, I was astounded at how she picked up on patterns in my possessions (like my attraction to royal blue and calla

---

[31] *The topic of my cats no doubt could serve as a psychological assessment for someone. It's a long story, but after I moved back to Illinois, one of my nieces was volunteering at an animal shelter and guilted me into adopting a cat. Then, I was spending a lot of time working with a rather driven partner on some matters related to proposed regulations that came out of the Sarbanes-Oxley Act of 2002. Turns out she had two cats and she insisted I get a second cat as a companion to the first, to the point she was going to ship me a cat. So, I adopted another cat. Accounting nerd that I am, it should surprise no one that I named them Banes and Oxley.*

lilies), how I had picked up artwork on my travels. She suggested adding elements to make the apartment more infused with natural elements to make it a bit cozier. I hired her to start the transformation.

Meanwhile, an e-mail was circulated asking partners in my group if any of us might be interested in doing a strategic international assignment for a few years in countries like China, Australia and Russia. I immediately raised my hand. The Chinese economy was going like gangbusters and, in both China and Russia, there was plenty of work in my area since they ranked high on Transparency International's Corruption Perception Index and the U.S. government was pursuing numerous investigations in both. Australia was pretty far out there, but why not?

I didn't hear anything back, so I assumed that either they had found someone else with a better skillset or fit to their needs or that, with the start of the subprime financial crisis that would lead to the Great Recession, perhaps the timing was no longer right for such assignments. Imagine my surprise several months later, then, when I got a question out of the blue as to whether I might be interested in a three- or four-year assignment in Germany.

*Oh. That wasn't on the list. But it's much closer than Australia and China, I know a bit about the country as I spent a couple months there for a project some years back and, well, one part of my Euro mutt ancestry **is** German….*

"Why, yes. Yes, I *am* interested," I told them.

And then, once again, crickets.

Hmmm….

139

And then just before Thanksgiving, I got news that it was on and, um, yeah, I needed to be there on January 1.

.   *Wait, what? Like in six weeks?!*

Yes. And I nevertheless accepted it, pretty much sight unseen. I did have a short trip over there to meet my boss and start hunting for an apartment in early December, but that was about it. The final touches were made to my condo a few weeks later, I enjoyed it for about two weeks, had a big party in the updated digs, and then the movers came. And I was off to Germany. On my own.[32] With a literal one-way ticket.[33]

It sounds exciting, right? And it was. But it was also really scary and intimidating when I started thinking about what I had gotten myself into. Actually, living on your own in another country is a whole lot different than staying in a hotel, taking taxis or trains wherever, eating at great restaurants or room service – basically having everything handed to you on a silver (or at least shiny chrome) platter. I didn't have the luxury of swinging through my condo in Chicago to feel the normalness of it all. I didn't have one of my teams from the U.S. that I'd worked with numerous times

---

[32] *Actually, Banes and Oxley joined me for the adventure, but they came a few months later (accompanied by one of my brothers and his wife with whom the cats stayed in the interim) after I was able to move into my apartment and had some furniture and things in place.*

[33] *Fun fact. I made Million Miler status on American Airlines on that flight. Likely because of that (though they didn't say it at the time), a woman came to the gate, summoned me to the podium via the PA, invited just me to pre-board, and escorted me onto the plane. I wasn't sure if I should feel like some kind of airline royalty or a VIP or that someone was making sure that I was really leaving the country. No turning back now! And yes, I had a glass of champagne before take-off, but no Mom to help me celebrate this time.*

and knew well. In fact, no one in our German practice knew me. I had no local experience, let alone a reputation there, positive or negative, though it was entirely possible that they'd heard rumors from speaking with European colleagues with whom I had worked on projects. Oh – and I didn't speak German.

One thing that I thought would be helpful was that I worked at the same firm, so we had the same values and everything, right? Yes, but values appear different when filtered through the prism of local culture and practice. The logo at the top of our letterhead looked the same[34] and some of the systems were the same, yet in many ways it was totally different because, well, things are done differently in Germany (and in any other country). So, it was similar, yet not. Just enough to make it confusing and decrease one's confidence and comfort level.

The idea of comfort is key when it comes to international assignments. While I can't speak about how things work at other organizations, when we ask our people to take international assignments, it's not a perk just given to someone as a reward for something. Nor do we send underperformers abroad to get rid of them. Quite the

---

[34] *Well, almost. The letterhead also indicates the legal name of the firm. The U.S. firm was simply the firm's name followed by LLP (for limited liability partnership) . . . I was a bit surprised to see the name of the German firm – the name followed by Wirtschaftsprufungsgesellschaft GmbH. Wait, did someone's cat step on their keyboard? When I asked what that was all about, colleagues explained that it was easy – just break the long word up into its components. Well, that's easier said than done when your vocabulary primarily consists of "Ein bier bitte." So, if you're interested, the cognates are Wirtschafts, prufung and gesellschaft, which mean, respectively, enterprises, examination, firm – or, basically, "auditing firm."*

contrary. International assignments are not cake walks, as I learned. They are also expensive, as the organization must pay for moving expenses, cost of living adjustments, tax equalization, visas, costs for expat employee children to attend the local international school, and other costs and benefits. So, we generally only do them for a strategic need that cannot be met in the local firm in the near term. And we select high performers who we are confident can get the job done, whatever that job is.

So, take a high performer, plant them in a new location, and they'll continue to grow and immediately deliver at the same level, right? Well, think about that. One reason the individual was likely successful in her home country was that she had a support network and infrastructure. Friends, family, trusted colleagues, a home, a car or accessible public transportation, financial accounts, the favorite grocery store, functional Internet and cable – you know, the stuff we take for granted. So, when you rip that person from her roots and put her in a different location – especially one where she doesn't speak the language – it takes a while to start to put those in place.

So that's the situation I was experiencing. For the first month or so, I was staying in a sort of long-term hotel room – a hotel without fancy amenities, but with a small kitchen and living room. Except I hadn't figured out where a grocery store was (ignore for now that I would be buying everything based on a German-English dictionary and pictures on boxes when I got there). There was cable, but everything (including *Law & Order* – don, don!) had German voice-overs (not subtitles, actual voice-overs so you couldn't hear the original English). There was good high-speed Internet, which was nice, but Netflix didn't work in Germany. I had a rental car whose GPS was set to German, which I discovered when I left the office late that first day and everyone else was gone. And then I couldn't figure out how/where to buy gas as I didn't see any in the city near the hotel nor did I see any along the way to the office. Just a few examples, but you get the idea. And at the same time, I needed to quickly get up-to-speed and start contributing and leading my new team. No pressure. Oh, did I mention that the recession was now in full swing? So, actually, yes, there was a LOT of pressure.

As I started to get my feet wet at work, one of the most immediate concerns was establishing my home in Frankfurt. Our office is in a suburb outside of town, but I wanted to live in the city where I could take advantage of concerts, shopping and all of that. And I was certain that I didn't want to live in some fancy frou-frou expat enclave where everyone spoke English. No, I wanted to live in a typical Frankfurt neighborhood with a bit of style and history, so I chose Sachsenhausen. I could walk or take the subway or tram to the city center, as well as trains or buses to the airport. There were great restaurants, many of which featured *apfelwein* (apple wine)[35] served in the iconic Bembel blue patterned earthenware jugs. And the neighborhood had a bunch of gorgeous, really old (from an American perspective)

---

[35] *It's an acquired taste. Served hot or cold or sometimes mixed with sodas or something, I was apparently not there long enough to fall in love, other than with the Bembel pottery pattern.*

buildings. I had this big dream of living in one of them and did look at a few. But that's when I started noticing two things about apartment living in Germany.

First, apartments there do not come with things we consider standard in the U.S. For example, in the U.S. your apartment has a kitchen that, if you're renting, usually includes appliances. In Germany, there is a room FOR the kitchen, but you supply all of the appliances AND all of the cabinets. What?! Yeah. And then you may have to rip it out if the next tenant doesn't want it because he's bringing his cabinets and appliances from his old place. This makes noooooo sense to me, but people also live for extended periods of time (we're talking decades) in their apartments, so I guess it does make a certain amount of sense to customize it to your own taste. Similarly, while a room in the U.S. must have a closet to be considered a bedroom, there are generally no closets in a German home. Instead, you must design and buy your own free-standing closet system, pay to have it installed and, like the kitchen, rip it out if the next tenant or the landlord doesn't want it. Can't make this stuff up.

The other thing about apartment living in any large city is that it's often really difficult to find street parking and not many buildings have designated parking places. So I ended up choosing a new construction apartment that had underground parking and an attached Rewe supermarket that was open rather long hours (for Germany), had a lot of sunshine and gorgeous hardwood floors, had no air conditioning (but it's new construction!!!), was fancy enough to have an elevator, and featured two apartments on each level. The only complication was that, because it was new construction, it wasn't yet available to move in. So, I had to live in the hotel until the apartment was available. It became available in February and even though my furniture shipment from the U.S. hadn't arrived yet, I couldn't wait to get out of the hotel (despite their very tasty breakfast). So, I headed to IKEA, bought a cheap mattress and some lamps[36] and started to camp in my new apartment.

I worked up the courage to go across the street to a store that sold appliances, televisions, coffee machines and other necessities. Like a Best Buy without personal electronics. Recall that I didn't really speak German. But I sallied forth and met Barney. This poor, lovely man. He was soooooo patient with me. But I think he realized I'd probably buy whatever he put in front of me. That first visit it was a small television. Then a (one of my favorite German words) *staubsauger* (vacuum). Later I went back for a Nespresso machine. And another for the office. And a larger television for the living room. He was even kind enough to come over and set up the first TV since I clearly had no clue how the satellite service that was included in my apartment rental worked or how to access it.

That Sunday night found me sitting on my EUR 25 metal-framed nylon-covered IKEA rocking chair, rocking on

---

[36] *Another, er, "feature" of German apartments is that they do not include lighting fixtures. At all. Not even a socket dangling from the ceiling exists. Nor lights around the bathroom mirror. You have to buy it all. So, the first couple of weeks, I was dragging that darn lamp all around the apartment, including into the bathroom. Ever try to fix your hair or put your make-up on with lighting from a floor lamp? It wasn't pretty. And neither was I.*

a piece of cardboard to ensure I wasn't making noise or marks on the floors, and watching said television with rapt attention and a German-English/English-German dictionary at the ready. And then I heard a knock on the door.

Uh oh.

One of the things the firm did before I left the U.S. was to give me a one-day crash course in cultural sensitivity training.

Seriously? I mean, Germans are like us, right? And I am of German ancestry, so....

Using one of my favorite German non-words, *jein* (yes and no).[37] There are some fascinating aspects of German culture. Among other things, according to the training, Germans keep to themselves. You may live years in a building and not really know your neighbors and will still be calling them Frau and Herr (whatever the name is on their nameplate on the apartment exterior). Oh. And there are rules about noise restriction and what you can do on Sunday, especially as Sunday is a big family day. So, as I sat there that Sunday night with someone knocking on my door, my immediate thought was, "Oh no! Someone can hear my television through the floor on family day!"

Oh, no. Oh, no. Gonna be angry Germans at my door and I can't speak German to apologize....

Channeling the best of Rosetta Stone, I opened the door and found two young women there holding a plant and their personal cards. They smiled – good and unexpected start – and launched into a rapid stream of German and I had

---

[37] *It is a contraction of the words for yes ("ja") and no ("nein").*

to rudely interrupt with the apparently-universal time-out sign. Fortunately, they spoke English. They were the neighbors living in the other unit on my floor. And, contrary to everything I learned in the cultural sensitivity training, they opened up their home and hearts to me, invited me to participate in many things I wouldn't have experienced otherwise, and showed me true German hospitality. They also became my best friends in Frankfurt as well as my go-to people to try to understand what had happened in various situations along the way that I hadn't quite figured out. The three of us remain friends to this day.

So, let me pause here and review where my life success factors were at this point in time. In short – nearly nonexistent except for active exploration. I'm not sure even that was working for me because I certainly wasn't choosing what I was learning, but just trying to tread water to figure out what was going on and how to live in Germany (kind of like having to read so much while in law school). Other than my AMAZING neighbors, I didn't know anyone outside of work, didn't have a team and had little interaction with my friends and family unless my blog counted. Creativity? Ha. Health? Double ha. Financial stability? With currency adjustments and trying to figure out what I was being paid where, also a bit up in the air. So, in comparison, the ridiculous year and months leading up to making partner – when I HAD some level of support structure – seemed like a breeze by comparison.

I was drowning. And wouldn't you know it, someone threw me a lifeline, albeit one cleverly tied to an anchor that threatened to pull me further under.

Because of the recession and economic downturn, we weren't able to promote anyone in our practice in Germany to partner that year. One of the candidates, who was leading our nascent forensic technology practice, left after he learned he wouldn't be promoted that year. My boss asked if I would be willing to step in and manage the practice while we searched for someone else to fill the role as the forensic technology manager was not quite ready to assume the leadership role.

"Manage as in just see the current projects to completion, or try to actually build the practice?" I asked.

He looked at me with a puzzled expression. "Well, if you were going to build the practice, you'd need to have forensic technology experience, so...."

*Hmmmm.... If I disclose that I actually spent several years working in forensic technology, including computer forensics, data analytics and electronic discovery, would that potentially be taking a step backward to something I left behind? Or can I use that admittedly dated experience to be able to pitch in and help the practice and feel a bit like I, well, **belong**?*

So, I told him that I actually *did* have that experience and would be happy to try to get things under control and help the manager further develop the practice while my boss worked on hiring someone new. He seemed both surprised and happy that, at least in the short term, the problem was solved.

Make that in the *very* short term because the practice somewhat unexpectedly won a huge project that required extensive use of forensic technology and electronic discovery (eDiscovery) services and capabilities. Unfortunately, because we hadn't had many other projects, we had agreed to let the forensics technology manager be put on a long-term assignment in a different country and we couldn't claw him back. We had bought an expensive new eDiscovery platform, but it wasn't fully installed in the top-secret data center in Germany and, well, no one really knew how to use it.

I stewed a little bit about this and pretty quickly did what anyone who was scared would do – phoned home. Not literally, but to some colleagues in the U.S. who had some idea of what all this entailed. This is where I saw how time I had spent supporting others and building relationships was repaid many times over. A partner in Texas, Eric, heard about my issues, called me up, and volunteered to send over some of his best team members to help and to even provide assistance himself if necessary. Colleagues in Poland who I had met while working on investigations there also volunteered to come over and help. And they looped in a colleague in Switzerland where, for data privacy reasons, our practice had their own installation of the fancy eDiscovery software and also spoke German. I was totally overwhelmed by the outpouring of assistance (and then by the mountain of paperwork and political feather-smoothing that would be required). I hired a few entry-level team members in Frankfurt to support those other professionals as well as to learn so that they, along with the manager who I was desperately trying to recall from the long-term project, could carry on and let the other professionals return home when things got to a calm place.

In a nutshell, I had my team. Even if I was borrowing some of them.

They.

Were.

AMAZING.

I am still so incredibly proud of all that they did under very stressful conditions. And also, under not-so-great actual work environments. For example, Germany doesn't have hot summers (compared to most of the U.S.) and, either because of that or a general aversion towards the artificiality and draftiness of air conditioning, our office and most homes did not have air conditioning. Our office had an "air cooling system" that, um, did only a moderate job of cooling. The office windows did open, though, so you could get some cooler air in early morning.

There was also a system of large metal vertical blinds (each blade was at least three inches wide versus the inch or so that's more common in the U.S.) in the 6-8 inch gap between the inner and outer windows that, when the sun hit a certain way or something, would automatically descend via motors and close in a manner and darkening effect that I can only analogize to the Batmobile armoring itself in the movies. You know, how the armor just comes around like a protective shell that looks somewhat like an airport baggage carousel on steroids? Like that. The first time this happened, I felt like I had suddenly been locked down in a prison. But thank goodness the internal door still worked! Those metal blinds and the separate window panels did keep things slightly cooler.

Anyway, take a generally warm condition on summer days, turn a couple offices into a lab, and have something like 10 laptops and servers working in that area without air conditioning and it got really hot, very quick. These poor guys (and a few gals) took it in stride and tried to come up with fun ways to try to make floor fans work better and, only after they thought I had already left for the day, took the uncommon (at least to Germans) step of stripping off their dress shirts and working in t-shirts. Fine by me!

While they were working in these sweatshop-like conditions, I had the job of running interference with the client, the law firm, the investigative team and others. That also included explaining where we were with collection and processing of electronic evidence and the numbers of "hits" we had from search terms in the documents so far. This role led to one of my most pivotal moments in my time in Germany.

I had a lot of experience with eDiscovery in general and this tool in particular from investigations I worked on when I was based in the U.S. I may not have been an expert at how to operate the tools, but I understood the overall process, the output, and how it changed as we added more data to the system.

In a typical investigation, you will have a number of individuals who may have information about the subject of the investigation. We might start an investigation with a few individuals in mind and, as we performed interviews with counsel or reviewed documents, we might identify additional individuals. Each of those individuals was considered a custodian. He might have information that could be shared via an interview, have printed files or documents or have information in digital form. The digital information could be in the form of e-mails, document files (such as Excel, Word, PDF), text messages, photos and videos, for example. That information could exist in a variety of places including laptop hard drives, network files, cloud storage, removable media such as USB drives or DVDs, or even mobile phones. Part of the investigation included identifying which of these sources were used by a particular custodian and then determine which information should be gathered.

The process of gathering the information was also important as each must be forensically secured to ensure the data was not modified and the chain of custody maintained from the time the data was acquired until the point at which it might be admitted as evidence in a legal proceeding. If you've watched many episodes of even television legal shows like *Law & Order* or *CSI,* you are no doubt familiar with this concept and what can happen if it's not followed.

Once the data was acquired, it then needed to be loaded into our eDiscovery platform so that it could be reviewed. That process also included something called de-duplication. Let's say that a custodian named John sent an email to Jerry, Susan and Tom and copied Meredith. If each of those recipients were custodians and data was acquired from all of them, we would have a copy in John's sent mail as well as in the inbox or other folder of the four recipients (assuming it had not already been deleted and wasn't picked up on network backups that may also have been forensically secured and loaded). In addition, some might have the e-mail on their laptop as well as in the e-mail system on their mobile phones. So, you could have at least 10 different copies of the exact same e-mail and there would be little point in reviewing the same document 10 times. So, the eDiscovery platform would de-duplicate and store only one record, though note that it related to all five custodians.

Once the data was de-duplicated and available for review, the team could then apply search terms to the data to determine whether there were hits for areas of interest. Using the example previously related to the Cypriot entity, search terms might include the name of that entity, the name of the government official and his wife, the name of the government project that the company was hoping to win, etc., and the information could be flagged as being relevant or not relevant or whatever flags were defined by the client and counsel. Each hit would show where the specific phrase or word was, and also identify related documents. For example, a search term might be in an email which also contained attachments, so the system would group all of them together so that the hit could be seen in proper context. I am greatly simplifying, but you get the idea.[38]

---

[38] *If you happen to be interested in more information, I recommend doing an internet search for the Electronic Discovery Reference Model or EDRM that provides an excellent overview of the processes involved in identifying relevant information.*

As you can imagine, the process of locating and forensically acquiring all of the data from all of the custodians takes time, and then loading into the system and de-duplicating and performing other processing takes additional time. Throughout the investigation, as new custodians and data sources are identified, the process is repeated and the amount of data available on the eDiscovery platform continues to increase.

I was used to this process, but the experience was relatively new to most of my colleagues in Germany. This wasn't because I was special or smart, but because the German legal system is totally different than the U.S. legal system, so there was little reason they would have been familiar with this U.S. approach to investigations. The U.S. system is an adversarial process where both sides of a matter have their own lawyers who zealously advocate on behalf of their clients. There are also rules that allow one side to compel the other side to produce relevant information through the discovery process. The German system doesn't have that type of discovery, so it was, literally, a foreign concept to many on the extended team.

So, as the matter progressed and more and more information was being analyzed and the numbers of documents and hits continued to change, there was a fair degree of confusion and frustration. At one point, my boss asked me to meet with him and a senior manager on the project to go through the latest reports. As I did so, he became frustrated and angry and began to raise his voice. This was uncharacteristic of him and I asked if he'd prefer to discuss the matter separately (because – ahem – it's generally not a good idea for two partners to argue in front of a subordinate, kind of like how it's often not a good thing for parents to argue in front of the children as it creates confusion, uncertainty and anxiety). But no, he wanted to continue.

Okay....

I tried to diffuse his frustration by explaining as calmly as I could what was going on and that it was entirely normal as we added new custodians and related data. But I cautioned that in order to maintain compliance with established protocols and processes, it was necessary to produce collection of documents in a certain way rather than to be selective, to include both the document with the hit as well as any other attachments or related documents.

And then he cut loose.

He stood up, color rising in his face, started pointing at me and yelling at me as the stricken senior manager watched very nervously.

"I don't know what *you people* do in the U.S., but here in Germany, we have *intelligent* professionals and I trust them to do know what they need to do. We don't need some *American* here telling *us* what to do! And in English, no less!" He practically spat out the English part.

[GULP]

Uh. So, I sense some animosity....

[PAUSE]

[CRICKETS]

I can hear the sound of my heart pounding in my brain. I want to yell back but that probably wouldn't help. But he clearly doesn't get it.

[DEEP BREATH]

Just be calm and let logic speak.

"Okay. So, if I understand you correctly, you're not concerned about not doing our best work for our client because you are okay with some members of our team remaining ignorant about how eDiscovery works?"

If I thought he was angry before, he was pretty much on fire after hearing that. I realize now that it was more provocative than I meant, not to mention that I said it in front of the senior manager who was still in the room which might have been embarrassing for my boss, but I had unfortunately already said it. Still pointing at me, he says, "**You cannot speak to me like that!!** I am the **leader** of this group. I *built* this team. And you have *no idea* what you are talking about!"

I'd like to say I had a calm comeback, but he and his shouting were getting to me. Flight or fight had been triggered and perhaps the years of law school gave me some hitherto unknown backbone and I decided to fight. My playground response was, "No, **you** have no idea what you're talking about! I'm a lawyer. When it comes to eDiscovery requirements, I know *exactly* what I'm talking about."

"Ja, an **American** lawyer," he sneered.

"Right! Because we're talking about *U.S. law*." I'm sure my face was red by this time as well. My initial shock at his words was quickly being overcome by anger. And I also knew that I was right.

He switched to German and I'm pretty sure he was swearing at me, but my German lessons didn't cover swearing, so I had no idea what, exactly, he said. Only that he was furious. And then he started talking to the senior manager there, apparently trying to get her to take sides. This clearly was not going to turn out well.

[DEEP BREATH]

I finally interrupted them, saying, "Look, it's clear that we disagree. Let's consult with a neutral party to determine how we move forward. I'm happy to be proven wrong on this, but we need to ensure that we serve our clients according to our professional standards and firm policies. As the leader of the practice, would you like to call the appropriate individuals, or would you like me to start that process?"

He just glared at me. And motioned for me to leave, as if waving away a bothersome fly. I had been dismissed. In multiple ways.

So, I left the conference room. After the initial argument and rush of adrenaline, I tried to calm down. My heart was racing. It took at least an hour for my hands to stop shaking. I didn't know what I should do next, but it was already evening, so I just left the office and went back to my hotel room.

And called the appropriate individuals. There were some very tense and awkward conversations over the next couple of days and, um, it turned out I was right.

But it was a pyrrhic victory as I was concerned that my relationship with my boss might be forever changed, and not for the better. And he did have a point – he **did** lead the practice, so he could do what he wanted. Up to a point.

The experience took a toll on my self-confidence and I really started to second-guess myself. Had I done the right thing? Is it possible to be insubordinate when we're both partners? Could he fire me and send me back home? Could this have a negative impact on my team, in terms of limiting their opportunities if mine were limited or feeling anxious because of all of the tension?

I felt really, really alone. While that was somewhat the case already just living in Germany without my support network, this was a step further. I didn't really have anyone I *thought* I could talk to. I didn't want to call friends or colleagues back in the U.S. for fear they would think I was weak or not able to handle being abroad or whatever. Which is silly, of course. In fact, I've shared this story with some people and without exception, the reaction was, "OMG. Why didn't you call me?!" And they apparently feel bad that I didn't feel comfortable reaching out to them, which would be my reaction as well if the situation were reversed. But I was so deep in my own funk I couldn't react, couldn't process, couldn't think beyond myself let alone – this is my whole point of telling this story – how I could move forward with my life vision.

Even though I was "right," I somehow thought that I had failed. What, just because my boss yelled at me?

Yes, lame as that sounds to me now.

But what I started to realize is I hadn't lost; I had just grown. When the going got tough, my years of training on the firm's values and policies kicked in. Things like, "We have a culture of doing the right thing." And, "When in doubt, consult, consult, consult." And that's exactly what I had done. And we got to the right answer for our client and the firm. So, there was no reason to feel like I had somehow lost.

And more importantly, I had survived. I hadn't been through that type of experience before, but now I had. I'd come out on the other side just fine. And I decided I wanted to remind myself of that. So, the weekend after that experience, I did what many ladies might do – I went shopping.

I bought a Wellendorff ring. I hadn't heard of Wellendorff until I lived in Germany and still don't see many of them in the U.S. Their unique offering is a spinning ring where the outer layer of the rings spins around. A ring that's made to be played with, in essence.[39] It's mesmerizing. Most have very intricate designs and are a bit over-the-top for me, but I bought the 2010 ring of the year that seemed particularly fitting as it was for "a special lady who listens to her mind and heart," which sounds a lot like someone who has some life success factors. Whenever I wear it, I look at it and celebrate how I have succeeded and grown through difficult experiences. And I'll often wear it when I expect a challenging day or situation as it's a sort of talisman to keep me focused and moving forward.

---

[39] *A fidget spinner has NOTHING on Wellendorff.*

Life will throw you curveballs. Even if you're living a life guided by your life success factors, it will not be a smooth path. And if it is, you're probably not challenging yourself enough. When you have a life vision, you can try to manage the process. But if you could just snap your fingers and be there at the life vision, you wouldn't *need* a life vision. You have to work to get there. You have to set intermediate goals. You have to work towards them. You have to try things you've never done before.

When you put yourself out there and try something new, you make yourself vulnerable and it can sting when you're not perfect – or fall flat on your face. But you grow through that. And it will almost always seem worse to you than what the reality is. Case in point, I thought my relationship with my boss in Germany was possibly irreparably damaged. But it wasn't. I'd caught him on a bad day. There were a few difficult days as we worked through the issue, but we moved on and things got better. Yet at the end of the year when I was receiving my performance review from him, I was still a bit nervous. Would there be lasting fallout from that one interaction? Would it overshadow what I had done throughout the year?

We were unfortunately doing the review via phone rather than in person, which always makes things a bit more difficult in terms of reading the other person. He asked me to start out by summarizing how I thought my year went and what I thought my annual rating should be. He paused (which pause was magnified via phone) and said, "I disagree."

Uh oh. This might be worse than I thought it was going to be....

Imagine my surprise, then, when he said I deserved a better rating. I had joined the practice at a really unfortunate time with the recession hitting, not being able to promote some of the senior managers and it really only being the two of us as partners. "And look at what we did, SanDee! We had the best year ever. And that was you and me. As partners. I could not have done this without you." And then he asked if I might consider extending my stay.

I was nearly speechless but finally found words to say thank you, that I appreciated the feedback and that I was glad that we had been able to work through some of the, er, difficulties earlier in the year.

As I let the review and that conversation sink in, I realized how much I had overreacted both in the moment and in the days and weeks afterwards. I assumed the worst intentions of a fellow partner who was also my boss based on one heated exchange and I was just totally wrong. I had continued to carry anxiety about one event whereas he had just moved on. Part of this may be a difference between how men and women operate, but it also serves as a reminder that when we're in the midst of a struggle, it's easy to get sucked into thinking only about that moment and to blow it out of proportion. It can be difficult to see past the struggle to the longer term and how that one moment might be a mere blip on the screen. It is precisely when we feel we are under attack that we need to steal just a brief moment, re-align to our life vision so that we know the direction we need to move, one stumbling step at a time.

When you choose to put yourself in a situation where you're trying something new, it will be hard and will take a lot of work. This is particularly when, as was my case, I didn't have strong relationships with those who were on the same project. You will fail at some things. You just will because no one is perfect.

Think of anyone highly successful in life – someone who strikes you as being at the top of their game, whether it's in music, sports, professional life, being a parent, whatever. I guarantee you they have all had to work to get there and have struggled along the way and, yes, failed. Sure, maybe Michael Jordan may have had some aptitude for basketball, but even he faced struggles. In high school, he tried out for the varsity basketball team his sophomore year but was deemed too short. So, he worked hard to improve his skills on the junior varsity team and, fortunately, grew four inches that year and was able to join the varsity team the next year. And then he lived happily ever after, right? But wait, what about his retirement from the NBA and foray into minor league baseball where he was not very successful? He put himself out there, tried, and realized that his interests were still more aligned to basketball and he returned to the NBA. We consider him a champion because he persisted, not a failure because he tried something that didn't work out for him.

Or take Carly Fiorina, who worked her way up through Lucent Technologies and went on to become CEO of

Hewlett-Packard. She was the first woman ever to lead a Fortune 20 company, so I was fascinated by this news at the time as a young professional. And then she was very publicly fired six years later. But she picked herself up and, after battling breast cancer, ran as the Republican candidate for U.S. Senate from California.[40] And lost. And then she ran for President of the United States in 2016. And lost again. And she continues on, lending her skills to various philanthropic organizations. One cannot help but admire her courage to keep putting herself out there and not give up.

A few other examples:
- Bill Gates and Paul Allen's Traf-O-Data device failed and so did the company.
- Jerry Seinfeld tried open mic night, froze and forgot his joke and was booed off stage.
- J.K. Rowling considered herself a failure, suffered from clinical depression, and her book about a wizard was rejected by all 12 major publishing houses.
- Madonna was fired from Dunkin' Donuts and robbed at knife point on the streets of New York while barely eking out an existence as a dancer.
- Mark Cuban failed as a bartender, short-order cook and computer salesman.
- Oprah was removed as a news co-anchor because the producer thought she was unfit for television.

---

[40] *I remain a bit traumatized by the "demon sheep" ad she ran during that campaign. It is available on the Internet, of course, if you would also like to experience that trauma. Skip to the end for the best parts.*

- Beyonce's first all-girl group, Girl's Tyme, lost on *Star Search*.

I could go on, but you get the idea. None of these people – and countless others – allowed a setback to keep them from pursuing their dreams. They stopped, dusted themselves off, and kept moving ahead.

A person who is just sitting at home channel-surfing through reality TV rather than engaging in real life can criticize you all they want, but they're not growing. **You are**. So, don't listen to them. Don't listen to any negative self-talk you may have. Look down at your Wellendorff ring type of reminder or play your life soundtrack or whatever works for you to remember how far you've come. How much you have grown. How amazing you are. And then focus on taking the next step toward your life vision.

One of the things that I have found helpful to keep focused on my life vision is to think about my life vision three years out, every single day. I wish I had started doing this years ago as it certainly would have helped me during difficult times. That visualization is part of my daily morning routine after I've walked through my calendar and blocked out time when I will attend to the three or so things, I must get accomplished that day. It only takes a minute or two, but I go through various aspects of my life and visualize as specifically as possible what I want my life to look like when that vision is realized. For me, this can range from topics like my career, my relationship with my nieces, mentoring, languages, travel, my home, my fitness level and what I eat and drink. I may focus on different topics on a particular day, but by visualizing on a regular basis what my life can look like, I build into my psyche that it will happen.

Then, thinking about what I have already laid out in my calendar, I visualize how I want that specific day to go from the time I finish that visualization exercise to the moment my head hits the pillow that night -- how each part would play out in a perfect world. As with the three-year visualization, when I create a positive intention for the day, how I will approach the events of the day and what I will make the time for, I greatly increase the likelihood that the day will go at least better than if I hadn't thought about it at all. It doesn't mean that some jerk won't cut me off in traffic. But if I've set an intention to be calm throughout the day and have a safe, relaxing commute to work while learning French, someone disrupting my commute doesn't take me off my game. I can still have a safe, relaxing commute and improve my language skills, and I have already decided that I will remain calm with whatever life throws at me (though I'll probably still honk the horn if it's deserved; I'm only human).

So, take some time to think about your life vision. Three years may be a good starting point, but if you have that set, you can also think about longer term horizons. There are a lot of great tools and techniques out there, such as vision boards or more focused assessments of areas of your life as in the online materials for Vishen Lakhiani's book, *The Code of the Extraordinary Mind*. Find what works for you, spend time creating the vision and revising it until it feels right.

Whatever your means of creating and reviewing your life vision, I encourage you to review and update it on a regular basis. If you create a formal life vision, I would recommend at least quarterly, comparing it to what you're visualizing on a day-to-day basis. Over time, it can and should change. By reviewing your vision and seeing how you have already progressed, you'll see how you're growing, where you want to grow more, what new things you want to include, and you can extend your horizon to focus on even more great things that you want to become your reality.

I've been doing this visualization and the periodic reviews for about a year while at the same time focusing more intently on goals to move towards that three-year life vision. And the interesting thing is how my daily visualizations have changed – because I have already made progress toward some of the things I was initially only visualizing in the three-year window. One of the things I visualized was being a published author. So, as I moved closer to the book being published, I had to enhance my vision around that area to think about what else is involved in being a published author, like book signings, speaking and perhaps working on another book.

For this and other areas, as I make progress towards the life, I re-set that part of the vision so that I always have forward momentum.

Chapter 9 – Re-aligning After Turns in the Road

"On days I feel like giving up, I look back and see progress I've made and realize the effort is worth it."

THE ROAD TO YOUR LIFE VISION is one of twists and turns. When you create your life vision, it seems like the course you're plotting is a pretty straight line. But life happens, your circumstances change, you adapt, and when you look in the rearview mirror, you see that you've had some bumps in the road and some amazing summits as well.

As I continued to work in Germany, I worked with my boss to hire someone to take over eDiscovery so that I could focus on forensic investigations and building out our practice in Frankfurt, as had been the original plan. As the years progressed, I developed a pretty decent support structure once again – not quite as familiar as back in Chicago, but I had friends, my German was better, I had local hang-outs and things I liked to do, had awesome neighbors, felt comfortable roaming around the country and Europe via plane, train, and automobile, and was generally getting the hang of living in Europe and loving it.

Time moved quickly, as it often does, and it was only about six months until I was to move back to the U.S. Even though I still had my condo in Chicago, it had been clear from the start that there wasn't a guaranteed right of return there.

As one of my clients who had done several tours abroad herself explained, when you repatriate, you need to do one of the following:

A. Have a new role
B. Go to a new location
C. Go to a new company
D. All of the above

Initially, I thought that was odd advice, but she explained that in an expatriate role, when you're re-creating your support structure and going through that exponential growth of figuring things out, your rate of growth is nearly exponential. But no one back at home really sees that. Yes, perhaps they see some things that you post on LinkedIn or social media and know you're doing something over there, but they tend to see you as you were when you left.

It's kind of like the annoying situation when I was a kid and friends of my parents who hadn't seen me for years would pat me on the head (sometimes also squeezing my cheeks, which I *reallllly* hated) and exclaim, "Oh, the last time I saw you, you were just a little bit of a thing...." And as I've gotten older, I've started to appreciate that because that's the last image they had in their mind. In the expat context, your colleagues will they think that they've grown a lot personally or professionally (for example, had a child or been promoted) but you're frozen in time for them at the point when you left. So, they think they've powered ahead of where you are – or at least where you *were*, as opposed to where you are now.

As I began discussing my return to the U.S., then, I was open to the practice's request that I head to New Jersey, since that's where so many of the life sciences companies are based. Made sense. I didn't really know much about New Jersey but had had a project in Princeton probably 10 years before and had been pleasantly surprised at how beautiful the state was once you got out of the Newark Airport area. Sign me up!

As I neared my last six months in Germany, I started researching places to live in New Jersey, learning more about the state and started to wind down or transition off of projects that I was leading. Then one of those sudden curves in the road of life appeared. Due to some health challenges, the partner leading our practice for the CIS region covering the Commonwealth of Independent States (Russia and 11 other countries) decided to resign. I was sad to hear that because I had always enjoyed working with him through the years. In addition, there was a lot of forensic accounting investigation work there because, well, Russia is quite high on Transparency International's Corruption Perception Index and U.S. authorities were stepping up investigations of American companies operating there, particularly life sciences companies.

You see where this is going, right? Our practice's leadership in Europe asked if I would step in to lead the group on an interim basis until they could hire a permanent replacement. Should only take six months or so, which would align with my return to the U.S. I would still be based in Frankfurt and could come home, say, every other weekend. I would be working out of our Moscow office, but also oversee a small team in Kiev; the two teams would travel to the other countries as necessary. The whole thing reminded me a bit of being asked to take over eDiscovery in Germany until we could find someone new, but I'd survived that, so what could possibly go wrong?

[SIGH]

The partner would be leaving in just two weeks, so I headed there as soon as I could get a visa so that I could have some time with him for a somewhat orderly transition. I arrived in early January and for a two-week period, the high temperature of the day did not exceed -20 Fahrenheit. I thought I knew cold, coming from Chicago, but I had no clue (and perhaps my blood had also thinned a bit in my years in Germany where the winters were very mild by comparison to Chicago). But the welcome was warm and the team very gracious.

A week or so into the transition, I was notified that in order for me to receive a longer-term visa to stay in Russia, I would need a work visa. And you can only have a Russian work visa if you have a contract with the firm in Russia. And you can't have a contract with both the German and Russian firms. And if you don't have a contract and work permit in Germany, then you can't have an apartment there, so....

Oh, no, no, no, no, no.... You said I could come back to my little happy place in Frankfurt every other weekend.

Yeah, actually, no.... And, well, since it's only an *interim* assignment, when you move out of your apartment in Frankfurt, we're just going to ship all your stuff to storage in

New Jersey and put you in a corporate apartment in Moscow with whatever you can bring over in suitcases.[41]

WHAT?!

At this point in time, it wasn't as if I could suddenly back out, but this was definitely not part of the plan. So just to recap, it was frigid January, I was being ripped out of my support network once again, I spoke no Russian, I'd be responsible for an entire practice covering 12 countries, and the cats and I would be camping out in an austere apartment with just a few suitcases of my clothing for company and comfort. Did I mention that there were also a whole bunch of violent protests and demonstrations going on in Moscow at the time?

Where's that Wellendorff ring?

It was certainly an, um, interesting experience. We were incredibly busy and working long hours and usually six days per week, which neither gave me time to pause and reflect nor allowed me to feel too lonely. Unfortunately, I also didn't end up seeing much of the region other than Moscow itself, St. Petersburg and Kiev. One older gentleman in our practice and his female friend took me under their wing and took me to some great museums, interesting restaurants,

---

[41] *I should note that the cats did not have to go into storage in New Jersey, which would've been an obvious deal breaker (I do have some limits). With the assistance of a pet relocation company (yes, that's actually a thing), the cats made it over and through cat immigration and arrived at the corporate apartment yowling and complaining that they needed better coats and perhaps tuques if they were going to be staying in Russia. I felt their pain. The corporate apartment people, incidentally, were less pleased about the arrival of the cats. When I came home one day, they had rolled up all the rugs and placed them in storage as apparently, they thought the cats would destroy them or something. So, I spent the rest of the time in an apartment with hardwood floors and no rugs. Not exactly cozy.*

organized a tour of subway stations from different eras and even helped me buy and ship a piece of artwork; I will always remember those times fondly. Overall, though, the experience was similar to that in Germany but with more chaos and slightly less drama. Slightly.

When it was finally[42] time to move back to the U.S., I was looking forward to everything being easy again. Except it really wasn't. Yes, I was in an English-speaking country, but I was in an area I hadn't lived in before, I didn't have family or friends there or a team and basically had to go through the whole support structure building thing again.

My client's advice about a new role, new location, new company or all of the above and the reasons for that came into clear focus as I tried to settle in. Even though I was in a new location, I was basically in the same role with the same practice and same industry focus that I had been before I moved to Germany, so not really all that new. And it was exactly as the client had predicted. No one really knew or understood what I had done and accomplished in my time in Germany and Russia. When I had left Chicago, I was a new partner and that seemed to be how everyone remembered me. That was despite my having not only led our practice in one of the larger offices in Europe, but also the practice (albeit on an interim basis) for an entire region, dealing with hiring, budgeting, performance assessment, practice management, team development, and marketing, in addition to serving our clients.

---

[42] *What was to have been only six months ended up being nine months and might have been longer, but I had put an offer on a place in New Jersey, so I insisted that I needed to move on and get my life started there.*

It felt like I had taken a huge step backwards in terms of developing my skills or using the expertise that I had developed. Like being told I had to crawl again after I'd learned how to walk, run **and** fly. It was incredibly frustrating and, well, also really boring. Not because there was nothing to do – far from it – but because all of the hard work didn't really seem to be something that would help me grow, either in the near- or long-term.

While I lived abroad, I had essentially been overdosing on active exploration, which provided a steady stream of both stress as well as energizing experiences that kept me engaged. In New Jersey, I only felt stress without the growth; it was the worst of both worlds – stress and stagnation verging on atrophy. And unlike Germany or Russia, there wasn't an end date that I could look to and just suck it up and power through this because something better was around the corner.

I understood that I had lost sight in Europe of some of my life success factors as active exploration had taken center stage. My health was, as usual, not great. My financial stability was fine. My creativity was okay as I'd applied it in doing different things with my teams in Germany and Russia and in some interesting projects and I was eager to test out those ideas in New Jersey. Imagine my frustration when I was told several times something to the effect of, "Well, that may have worked in Russia or Germany, but that's not how we do things here" or "They're not as sophisticated as our practice." How would they know?! My frustration grew.

One of my biggest mistakes during this time was not revisiting my life vision and instead just doubling down on the existing vision – working internationally and spending time with my teams that were spread across the world. I was trying to force that to work, even though my wings had essentially been clipped until I could reestablish myself in the U.S. and start selling some international projects. But I didn't take a step back and really think about whether that life vision made sense for me or what changes I needed to make.

I was in a different place in life, literally and figuratively. Despite the stress of essentially working without a safety net beneath me while I was in Europe, I had really enjoyed not flying around the world, but staying closer to the new definition of home and building teams. I liked creating a plan for what we wanted to accomplish in Frankfurt and CIS, and recruiting people to join that vision, whether new professionals joining the firm or existing professionals who I wanted to join me in forging a new direction. I reveled in watching the teams grow and our professionals take up increasing responsibilities and then, in turn, leading others. I loved how we were focused on identifying unmet needs at clients and helping them fill that gap and creating bridges to other parts of the firm at the same time. It was exhilarating.

THAT was part of my new life vision. I was also getting married to an amazing woman I had met in Switzerland, so that certainly changed what was important to me and should have been a clue to revisit the life vision. But instead of talking with her about my increasing unhappiness, I felt like I needed to act like I had everything under control – odd, given that she knew me when I was living in Germany and Russia and knew that I most certainly did **not** have life under control!

As I tried to get used to the new normal, though, I kept hammering away at meaningful relationships, including building new relationships with colleagues in the U.S. and getting back in touch with those I had known before I'd headed to Germany and (admittedly) may not have done that well at staying in touch. One of those was Ted, who had invited me to join his life sciences team years ago. He had advanced within the firm and was in a leadership position. He has an interesting and multicultural background and seemed to understand that I was missing the world traveler and explorer aspect of living abroad and feeling less than inspired.

He called me one day and asked if I remembered how we had talked about the importance of helping clients create effective compliance programs where Compliance became the Department of How rather than the Department of No?

Yes, of course.

And how it's important for compliance to be embedded within the organization and to have employees from the business side spend some time in Compliance to share knowledge both ways.

Sure…

"Well, how about doing a rotation in our Independence group here at the firm, which is essentially our version of regulatory compliance?"

Oh, I see what you did there. Clever. That just doesn't sound very interesting, though.

At the same time, though, Ted had never steered me wrong. So I agreed to think about it. I reached out to quite a few other partners to get their take on such a rotation. Would there really be a path back to client service? Would this be seen as some kind of career limiting move? But at the same time, it WAS something I had been helping clients with for several years. Our business as a firm continued to change with advances in technology and globalization, so that would undoubtedly have an impact on our regulatory obligations. And regulations are, of course, part of the law, so I could use some of my legal training (without practicing law, of course). It sounded like it might also be intellectually stimulating. And there certainly would be a lot to learn.

Hmmm....

I interviewed for the position and accepted the offer I received. And I liked it so much that I decided to stay after the rotation period, which I never would have anticipated. I do miss aspects of my previous position, just as we often miss things in our past when we move on. But I realize they're the part of a different version of me that I've outgrown, even as I have solidified my commitment to tuning in to all of my life success factors.

I've rediscovered *active exploration and teaching* as I'm now focused on an entirely new field of study. I learn something new each week (usually each day) and also have the ability to teach others, both in formal training sessions and through day-to-day consultations and interactions. My longer commute is allowing me to work on learning more languages and I've been able to schedule some interesting international vacations to continue that type of exploration.

In addition to a new team within the group, I have the opportunity to meet many more people than I likely would have in my client service position, developing *meaningful relationships* in different areas of the firm and in operations that I've had very little exposure to before. I've also found that colleagues in my former practice group have increasingly sought me out for career advice and mentoring as I understand their world but am far enough away to be objective and trusted. I feel like I missed some key years in the lives of my four nieces while I lived in Europe, so I'm also working on re-establishing relationships with them and my extended family.

Health, well, may always be a bit of a struggle for me, but I've developed some better habits and approaches to fitness and food that are having a positive impact on my life. I've started meditating and keep a daily gratitude journal and little things like that have helped me feel less stressed and more in control of my emotions and mental well-being and peace. Like all the other areas, though, there's always more work to be done.

My *financial stability* is fine. Yes, I will likely earn less over time if I stay in the current group, but my goal here isn't wealth but stability, so this works for me (I mean, don't tell my boss that – I still want raises, okay?).

And I can't remember – other than a few times in Russia that I'd not care to repeat – having so many opportunities to be creative at work. My position involves constant problem solving, working with teams that have questions, helping them find solutions, thinking about new services and what they may involve, and never being quite sure what may pop up in my email box or an instant message ping. Oddly enough, I enjoy that type of environment. And I have also started working in time in my off hours for more creative endeavors like practicing the piano, trying my hand at landscape design, developing ways to challenge our dogs, and, you know, things like writing my first book.

These haven't fallen into place by happenstance. It's because I re-evaluated my life vision and expanded it significantly to focus not only on my teams, but serving others, on low-key exploration, expanding my relationships with my loved ones, helping others on their journeys and finding more things that bring me joy and happiness.

I know that I made the right choice. For now. But this vision will change. Must change. Because I insist on growing, on seeing what's over the next hill, and sneaking a peek behind me every once in a while to see how far I've gone while skipping to the next track of my life soundtrack's sequel.

Chapter 10 – Pulling It All Together

"Challenge all habits – even good ones."

SO FAR, WE'VE DISCUSSED life success factors and how they can help guide you toward your life vision. The missing pieces, though, are the goals that you set to achieve the life vision and the habits you build to help you achieve those goals.

Not all of your goals may relate directly toward your life vision. For example, you may be at a time in life where your near-term goal is to just grind things out so you can move on to something better. For example, you want to afford gifts for friends and family, so you pick up a second job over the holidays. Even in many of those situations, the goals may relate to your life vision or possibly to your life success factors. For example, you're picking up the second job because meaningful relationships are important to you. Or you really despise a particular project at work, so you're just gritting your teeth and powering through to get it over with – and perhaps also so that you can return to the part of your job that you like and that will contribute to your overall career aspirations. You get the idea.

So, take a few minutes to think about aspects of your life vision that you want to achieve.

Table 3

Life Vision Element
[Example] Exploring a variety of countries, not just as a tourist but trying to really absorb the cultures and experience

Now take each of those and create one or more realistic goals designed to help you progress towards that life vision element.

Table 4

Life Vision Element	Goal(s)
[Example] Exploring a variety of countries, not just as a tourist but trying to really absorb the cultures and experience	[Example] Visit 20 countries or regions in the next 15 years, researching each in advance for culture, history and art, and seeking out unique places to stay that will allow for interactions with local residents. Plan trips in sufficient advance to be able to complete Level 1 of the local language, to the extent possible.

Once you have some of these larger goals, break them down into smaller goals – annual, quarterly, monthly, weekly, et cetera. Large goals can be so daunting that it's hard to feel like you have any momentum. Obtaining a college degree is a good example of this. If you only had a goal of, "Get a college degree," it could seem really intimidating. But if you choose a major, you can then plot out your courses and sign up for classes one term at a time, turn in your projects and papers, do your homework each week, and show up for every class and exam, there's a good chance you'll achieve that goal.

Table 5

Goal	Annual	1st Quarter	1st Month	1st Week
Visit 20 countries in 15 years	Identify 2 destinations Plan & visit first country Begin planning the second Learn language basics for both countries	Identify 1st destination & begin planning visit Buy or borrow book(s) related to the destination Begin language learning Begin researching the country	Select 1st country Identify books, movies, documentaries on culture, history & art Begin language lessons Determine best months to visit Decide whether to go as a tour or create own itinerary	Brainstorm list of countries & discuss with friends / family Research language & study the languages of potential countries Create language study plan Identify & buy or borrow book on the country's culture or history

Once you have done these for each element of your life vision, you can begin plotting them out. A large 12-month calendar that you can post on the wall or back of a closet door is helpful as it will allow you to see where you might have conflicts among goals or with other life events.[43] It will also be an ever-present and highly visible reminder of what you want to accomplish to help hold you accountable. It will also help with pacing your deadlines. If you start out on January 1, for example, with audacious annual goals and have deadlines or milestones in all your areas at the end of the month, you may feel stressed and overwhelmed. It's generally better to stagger them a bit so that you can keep up your momentum and so that you can get a little dopamine boost when you meet those milestones.

---

[43] *You can, of course, use digital or other smaller calendars. I happen to use both so that I have access to my goals at any time, but also am confronted with the overall picture on a regular basis. One drawback of a digital planner is that you have to proactively open it up. Yes, you can set alarms or reminders, but to see the overview of what you're doing over a long period of time, you need to remember to go into the app or device and often can only see one month at a time (or everything but in micro font).*

Celebrate Milestones

One thing you'll want to build into your plans and that master calendar are celebrations. When you set your milestones, think about how you will reward yourself if you achieve the milestone (and on time). It gives you an added reason to achieve the goal and lets you savor your achievement a bit more. These do not have to be big celebrations. They could be as simple as having dinner at a French restaurant after you've completed French Level 1. A deep tissue massage after running your first 10K. A weekend away to reconnect with your significant other after working hard to finish the first draft of your book. You can also link celebrations together – something larger when you've hit significant milestones in multiple life vision areas.

A critical link to achieving these goals is taking deliberate action to incorporate them into your daily routines. Much of this comes down to developing habits that support your goals. I've outlined a few things that have been helpful for me based on various courses I've taken and books I've read. There are lots of books and programs out there, so find what works for you and is motivating, always ensuring that they help you consistently touch on your life success factors.[44]

---

[44] *For goal tracking, I have tried a variety of planners. The one that has worked best for me at this point in time is the Self Journal from Best Self. It's a quarterly system with two pages per day and with weekly trackers. The High-Performance Planner from Brendon Burchard is also good, though I found that it required too much daily work that didn't resonate with me and could be overwhelming. I also preferred the smaller size of the Best Self program. I am not endorsing either of these; they're just examples that I have found helpful, though I still supplement with my own annual/quarterly/monthly/weekly goal tracker, gratitude journal and rolling To Do list. More well-designed planners seem to be coming out all the time, so keep your eye out for one that matches your needs.*

Plan Your Week

This may seem obvious from the paragraphs above, since we have already broken-down larger goals down into what you want to accomplish in a particular week. Individually they may not seem like that much, but things happen in a week and if you don't plan for when you will do these tasks, it's highly likely that you will end the week without doing most, if not all, of them.

I block out time on Sunday to review my progress on the prior week's goals and plan the new week's goals based on what remains in the monthly and quarterly goals. Obviously, monthly and quarterly you will need more time to update those goals as well. Looking at those weekly goals, look at your calendar and determine which day(s) you will tackle each of those goals. Then take it one step further and try to block out time during that day to accomplish the task(s).

Identify Your Top Tasks for the Day

Identify 3-5 tasks that, if you complete them, will make the day a success for you. These should be clearly defined and achievable without too much effort. For example, "Write a research paper" might be a bit much if you haven't started it, but a smaller task like, "Identify primary resources for research paper" might be easier.

I used to have a list of five tasks that I would target each day. I wrote them on an index card and often found that I would just carry the card with some items scribbled off onto the next day when I didn't complete them, which got a bit depressing. It also caused me to lower my expectations just

185

so that I could claim "success" at the end of the day. But I wasn't accomplishing as much as I needed to. So, I reduced the list to three tasks so that I had better odds of completing all of them and getting that dopamine rush from making the check marks.

To be clear, I also have running To Do lists for work and for my personal life so that I can keep track of all that is going on. The 3-5 tasks list isn't a replacement for that. On a day-to-day basis, one of the tasks usually comes from my weekly goals list and the others generally relate to events or interactions on my calendar or things from the running To Do list.

Find Your Most Productive Time of the Day

When you're planning your day, you want to schedule the most important tasks for the day during the time of day that will give you the highest return on your investment of time. This is *not* necessarily the time of the day you most enjoy. What you're looking for is when you can get the most done. I'm a morning person and generally wake up with lots of energy, but I have found that my best work is done in the office before most others arrive. So I head in early and knock out the big work projects for the day but try to leave at a reasonable enough hour that I can work on my personal projects in the evening. You might need to get kids off to school before you can be productive or can settle down better after a good workout.

For a week or so, check your progress throughout the day. It may even be helpful to set an alarm on your phone every 2-3 hours to see how productive you've been, what you've accomplished. Write that down and then compare after a few days to see if patterns emerge that can help you be more strategic when managing your calendar, especially when it comes to knocking out those top 3-5 items.

Leave No Empty Space on Your Calendar

Empty space on your calendar will be filled one way or the other. By taking control of your calendar from the start, you improve the likelihood that your day will be filled with things that matter to your progress. Schedule out your entire day on your calendar and try to stick to it. It's true that if you don't plan time to get something done, it probably won't get done. You can start by plotting out the appointments or deadlines you know you have to meet. Then look at your 3-5 tasks that you want to complete and add those. Add in time for habits you want to cultivate, like studying a foreign language, journaling, meditating, or heading to the gym as well as the basic things of life you need to do like commute or eat. Take a look at the time remaining in your day.

Create a Stop Doing List

It is often a struggle to find time in your schedule for new habits. But if you're not willing to make changes, are those new goals you're shooting for truly important? One thing I've found helpful is to create a Stop Doing list. Identify things you do that don't contribute to your life vision, may be otherwise unnecessary or where you could cut down the time you spend on them. That doesn't mean you can't do those things, but you can manage how often you do them or how much time you spend doing them to free up time for other activities.

When I started thinking about this, I realized one of the things I needed to stop doing – or stop doing as much – was sitting down to relax with my iPad. And then when I'd look up, I'd realize I had wasted half an hour playing Candy Crush and watching kitten videos on social media. I also had a tendency to plan on watching one episode of *House of Cards* only to realize I'd watch a couple of those and then move on to a couple from another show. And I wasted my morning commute. I also wasted a lot of time and focus by switching between tasks whenever a notification popped up on my phone or laptop.

Once I realized where my time was going, I was in a better position to change my habits to make room for better choices. I replaced Candy Crush on my iPad with Lumosity, which I do once a day to train my brain.[45] I limit both the time I spend on social media and the number of times I do so, focusing on creating content and having online conversations and interactions with my friends and family. I generally only watch Netflix when traveling and have substituted non-fiction reading. My morning commute is spent learning language and my evening commute is listening to an audiobook or an audio course or calling friends or family. And I disabled the notifications on my laptop and devices for

---

[45] *One of my biggest fears is Alzheimer's or dementia. For someone who values active exploration, teaching and meaningful relationships, this is terrifying. So if brain training helps stave that off, five minutes a day with this or other programs seems well worth it. It is also, of course, consistent with my health life success factor. But if you happen to know of any scientific studies about Candy Crush helping with one's mental faculties, please let me know....*

new e-mail and social media posts; they will all still be there when I want to access them. I realize I now sound like a total bore, but this really helped me free up time for the things that I'd much rather do. Notice, for example, how many of the replacement activities relate to my active exploration and meaningful relationships life success factors.

Track Your Progress

As the saying goes, "What gets measured gets done." In addition to periodic reviews of your goal to track your progress, include in your weekly planning the habits and tasks that you want to achieve and do more of. The things I track may vary from week to week, but often include at least one thing related to health (e.g. sleep, workouts, hydration), studying language a specific number of times per week, posting original social media content, meditating, writing in my journal. Whatever you choose to track, keeping a record helps hold you accountable as well as can help you show your progress.

Conclusion

*"Stopping and thinking is often the fastest way
to move ahead."*

YOU ARE CAPABLE OF ACCOMPLISHING amazing things in life. You are also capable of taking the path of least resistance (and energy). Both are true regardless of your family history, your level of education, your race, your bank account, your weight, your IQ or pretty much any other demographic factor that defines you as you. Rather, the difference in outcomes boils down to two things: choice and change.

When you identify your life success factors, you *choose* to focus on what makes you happy and fulfilled. When you create a life vision, you *choose* to grow and strive and become a better version of yourself. When you apply your life success factors, you *choose* which path will lead you to your life vision. And when you *choose* goals to advance you on that path, you *choose* to **change**. And when you *choose to change*, **you choose you**. Because change is hard. It's uncomfortable. It requires energy. It requires explaining to others why you're doing things differently and risking them laughing or teasing you. It requires focus. And it requires letting go of who you are now to embrace who you *will be*.

If change and growth were easy, everyone would be doing it. Instead, the majority of people are floating along and taking life as it comes. And let's be clear -- you can have a decent life by floating along; it just won't be a great life that satisfies and fulfills you.

I speak from experience. A little over a year ago, I had a great job, a happy marriage, a home in a spectacular location, great colleagues, the unconditional love of our dogs and cats,[46] a well-used passport, etc. I was happy on some levels but "meh" on many others. I decided that I wanted to, well, *be* more. I read some books, took some online courses, listened to a broader range of podcasts and started to make some small changes while doing some introspection along the way. I started adding little things to my day that became habits, like writing down what I was grateful for, pushing myself to try to meditate, fueling my body properly, creating a daily intention, focusing on how I invested my time and, of course, setting goals.

Yes, some of the changes were difficult. For example, instead of the 5 AM Club[47], I do the 4:30 or 4:15 AM Club – **nothing** about that was easy. But now, I wouldn't change it for the world because I start the day with so much energy and intention for the day. And as I started tracking my small goals, I could see my growth and how the habits started to settle in. And others could, too. I became more optimistic, calmer, patient, healthier, more confident and just – for lack of a better word – happier! I was becoming a better me – a me I much preferred to my old me, and I suspect was/is also preferred by my family, friends, colleagues and the strangers

---

[46] *Well, everything is conditional with cats, but you know what I mean.*

[47] *I mentioned Robin Sharma's book of the same name earlier. Another one with a similar premise is* Miracle Mornings *by Hal Elrod.*

in grocery stores who I now smile at because, you know, happy.

I thought that perhaps others might want to be happier, too, and that's how "author" became part of my life vision and how writing a book became a goal, guided by my life success factors of creativity and teaching. And here we are.

What I have tried to introduce in this book is a framework to help you create a satisfying and fulfilling life based on how you define both of those. But how that unfolds will be as unique to you as your life success factors. I've included some templates to help, but they're not a fancy methodology to adhere to, they're just a way to get you to start thinking about your life and what makes you happy. Feel free to create your own templates, to riff on any of the things I've created and improve upon them, as that would be the ultimate compliment to me – that I helped inspire you to create your future and how to get there.

And I'm still revising how I do this myself. When I was creating my annual goals at the beginning of this year, I thought, "Wow, that's a lot of goals. How can I try to organize them in some meaningful way?" Oh, duh, life success factors.

"But wait!" you may be saying. "I thought goals came out of the life vision and were guided by the life success factors."

Yes, they do, and they are. But because your life vision is something that will make you happy and engaged and satisfied, there's a good chance that those goals to get there will also track nicely to your life success factors. And then it's easy to see whether, in the year ahead, you're planning on attending to each of your life success factors.

Choice and change both require a significant amount of energy. But it is an investment that will pay dividends throughout the rest of your life if you choose to embrace the concepts as you have defined them for yourself.

When you choose yourself, you create the foundation for change. You must supply the energy to make the changes, but that energy will be returned in spades as you grow and lengthen your life vision horizon and prepare for each successive stage of growth.

Commit to yourself. Commit to change. Commit to an amazing life ahead.

Afterword

This is not the book that I expected to write. I have always thought it would be interesting to write a book but assumed that if I did so it would be a collection of odd stories that have happened to me at work and through my travels. But I met a fascinating and energetic author at a conference and ended up having lunch with her. As we talked, she opened my mind up to writing about what I was so clearly passionate about – personal development and coaching my peeps.

As an introvert, I'm not crazy about telling my personal stories – especially the not-so-great moments – and especially not publicly. But I realized that all of the things I have learned and that I think may be helpful to others are empty without sharing openly and authentically. So I started writing them.

While I was sharing those stories within the book, I also started sharing with friends, family and colleagues that I was writing a book in my "spare time." The first time I did so, I was somewhat apologetic. "I'd love to go to the movies, but I blocked out my time this weekend to write a chapter for my book."

"Your book? Really? That's cool! What's it about?"

So, I'd try to explain what it was I thought I was going to write about, even though the book hadn't yet been written. And they'd tell other people, who'd also ask about the book. And they'd ask how the book was coming, when it might be published and when could they get a copy to read. I was and remain overwhelmed by their support. And it made me feel even more comfortable talking about the book, especially with my counselees and mentees because I am confident the concepts can help them.

And that's the real next step: sharing your dreams with others. Taking the first steps of identifying your life success factors, creating your life vision and building the goals to move forward are critical. They will provide traction to get you moving in the right direction in an aligned way. But when you share them with others, most will enthusiastically urge you on. You will quickly see who your true supporters and friends are. And they might even join the journey with you.

Courage is contagious. And fewer things in life are more courageous than taking control of your life. Congratulations on taking that first step. I invite you to spread that contagious courage by sharing your life success factors (anonymously or by your name – up to you) at www.sandeepriser.com/lifesuccessfactors – to inspire and be inspired by each other.

Thank you for sharing your time in reading this book. I can't wait to see how life success factors help you move towards your own life vision!

Acknowledgements

One of my favorite discoveries in life is the unique skills, personalities, and passions of my "peeps" at work. They help bring out the best in me so that I can try to tease out the best in them. I'm not sure who may benefit more, but I am grateful for the opportunity to have worked with many women and men of different backgrounds, in different practices, in far-flung corners of the world, who hold a special place in my heart. You are truly building a better working world. And without you, I wouldn't have realized that I derive so much joy from helping others, nor given thought to writing this book to help others I have never even met.

As you can see from this book, I would not be where I am without the love and support of my Mom. We didn't have much, but she always managed to make sure that I had books, opportunities, and her unwavering support. I apologize in advance to everyone who visits her house, because she probably made you read this book. And then there are my brothers, who I appreciated for toughening me up for life, teaching me to be self-sufficient, and that the pen is mightier than the paring knife.

I've been blessed with amazing teachers and mentors throughout life. Mel Warner taught me the value of practice; Barbara Favorito encouraged me to stretch my wings and make the first of many moves to a new place; Bill Guska reinforced the value of family and laughter; Jay Layman showed me how networking works; Kathryn Oberly opened her busy calendar and vast experience to me as a young law student, and introduced me to Beth Brooke, who has encouraged me to think bigger and focus on mission and equality for all. All exemplify a mindset of giving back, and that's one of the best lessons I have learned from them.

"Writing a book" would likely have stayed on my "someday" list for many years had I not met author Michelle T. Lederman who asked questions and made me think about it seriously. She introduced me to her friends Sarah Fader and Adam Smith, who took me through a book coaching program that resulted in what is in your hands (or on your device). They, in turn, introduced me to the editing prowess of Wendy Garfinkle, who shepherded me through the publishing process with Emery Press Books. They have all been exceedingly patient with this newbie and her questions.

And none of this would mean anything without the support and encouragement from my wife, Kimberley, who gave me the time and room to write.

Finally, a special thanks to you, the reader, for listening to what I had to share. I hope to meet you online, if not in person, and hear about what may have resonated with you.

Appendix – Blank Tables

Table 1

Table 2

Life success factor	Relative importance	Past success (1-5)	Current status (1-5)	Gap (Past – Current)	Priority (Importance x Gap)

Table 3

Life Vision Element

Table 4

Life Vision Element	Goal(s)

Table 5

Goal	Annual	1st Quarter	1st Month	1st Week

CPSIA information can be obtained
at www.ICGtesting.com
Printed in the USA
BVHW041814100620
581272BV00005B/301

9 780960 050543